D1604587

MUSTANGS
A Return to the Wild

MUSTANGS
A Return to the Wild
By HOPE RYDEN

A STUDIO BOOK · THE VIKING PRESS · NEW YORK

Contents

Acknowledgments 7

Prologue: On the Track of the Wild Horse 9

Stallions 17

Young Stud Bands 27

More Stud Bands 35

Mares and Colts 41

The Plates 49

The History and Ecology of the Wild Horse 97

Notes to the Plates 105

References 111

To the Tillett Family
Who Fought for the Pryor Mountain Wild Horses

acknowledgments

I could not have photographed the wild horses without help and direction from many people who were familiar with the wilderness areas where wild horses still exist. In the Pryor Mountains I was given much assistance by Lloyd Tillett, Chuck Wagner, and the Reverend Floyd Schweigert. And when I was not up the mountains tracking mustangs, Lloyd and Abbie Tillett opened their doors to me and made me feel I had a second home. Whenever I became discouraged, their hospitality and belief in me kept me going.

In the Wassuk Range in western Nevada, Steven W. Pelligrini was kind enough to show me the horses he was studying for his thesis: "Home Range, Territoriality and Movement Patterns of Wild Horses in the Wassuk Range of Western Nevada." I not only wish to thank Steve for his help in the field, but also for his excellent study which I found to be extremely useful in analyzing my own observations.

Dr. Michael Pontrelli and Mrs. Velma Johnston (Wild Horse Annie) deserve special thanks for their dedication and continuing interest in wild horses.

It is reassuring to meet men in government service who have the high sense of commitment shown by Bureau of Land Management field workers Jim Brunner, David Walter, Malcolm Charlton, and Eddie Mayo. In helping me locate horses on the Nellis Air Force test site, these men extended themselves far beyond a perfunctory performance of duty.

I am especially indebted to the *National Geographic Magazine* for sponsoring two of my field trips while I was obtaining photographs to illustrate "On the Track of the West's Wild Horses" (*National Geographic Magazine*, January 1971). I am deeply grateful to Robert Gilka of the *National Geographic Magazine* staff who believed I would succeed, and to Dick Durrance, staff photographer, who accompanied me on the first field trip and taught me much I had not known before about the use of camera equipment.

Though it is impractical to list all their names here, I wish to thank the some one hundred Congressmen and Senators who sponsored legislation in the Ninety-second Congress of the United States to protect America's last wild horses. In particular, I am grateful to Congressman Walter S. Baring and Senators Henry M. Jackson, Mark O. Hatfield, and Lee Metcalf for helping to field this legislation through committee hearings and to a successful vote in both Houses.

I am grateful to my father, the Reverend E. E. Ryden, for reading sections of the text of this book and offering suggestions, and to Lewis S. Brown of the American Museum of Natural History for reviewing the manuscript before publication.

I also wish to thank Sid Reichman for lending me a spare camera, Jean Riss for her patience and help in typing the manuscript, and my editor Nicolas Ducrot for his enthusiasm and interest in wild horses in America.

Hope Ryden

PROLOGUE
On the Track of the Wild Horse

I first heard the sound of hoofbeats only seconds before the wild gray stallion began wheeling around me in perfect circles. He had appeared from nowhere, materializing out of blue haze and silence like some kind of desert phantom. But he was no mirage. The rhythmic thud of his drumming hoofs was grim proof of the reality of the animal who had me trapped within his orbit.

My fear was real too, and as the wild horse continued to circle me I began to grow dizzy, for I had to turn round and round just to keep him in view. The experience was not unlike riding the hub of a merry-go-round, except that the revolving wild stallion, who moved with so much action and grace, was no painted wooden steed; he was very much alive. Moreover, the giddy sensation I was experiencing was not a pleasurable feeling. I was in the middle of a Nevada desert, alone, and miles from cover.

Then, as if some unheard calliope tune had ended in his brain, the wild horse came to a stop, turned, and regarded me quizzically. I had managed to snap a few pictures of him while he was prancing around me, but now as he fixed his unwavering gaze upon me, my nerve failed. I stood with my arms hanging limply by my sides, my cameras dangling uselessly about my neck, trying my utmost to project passivity. I knew this was my best defense against arousing more aggressiveness in the wild horse.

I had been frightened by wild stallions before, and even menaced by them on occasion. During the three years I had spent tracking and photographing mustangs in remote habitats in the West, many stallions had made it clear to me that I was a trespasser in their isolated and inhospitable last retreats from man.

Normally, at the sight of an intruder a wild stallion stands his ground and faces the enemy while snorting a warning to his harem of mares to make their escape in the opposite direction. Then, after giving his females a few seconds lead-time, he, too, will depart at full gallop. However, on occasion, a particularly aggressive male would rush toward me, stopping only a few feet in front of me, and would put on a formidable display of belligerence. But I soon came to realize that even these provocative stallions would not hold me at bay for long, but would soon depart to join their females before the mares outdistanced them too far. The reason for this was obvious. Another stallion might be lurking in the vicinity, awaiting an opportunity to capture an unguarded harem.

But now I was confronted with a different situation. The gray stallion, who was eyeing me balefully, was a lone stud and had no mares to protect. Consequently, he would have no reason to make a swift departure. He might hold me captive all day.

I was curious to know why my presence on this wide-open desert should have antagonized a stallion with no harem to defend. I could only guess that he had been tracking the same little band of wild horses I had been trying to photograph all morning. The band was made up of a sorrel stallion, a gray mare, and a brown colt. I wondered whether my presence in the area had in some way interfered with the gray stallion's intention to ambush the sorrel stallion and abduct the gray mare. That, of course, would explain why I had not noticed him before—despite the fact that I had been scanning the desert landscape all morning for other mustangs. Like myself, he may have concealed himself by traveling in the draws, awaiting a propitious moment to attack the sorrel horse who at the moment was grazing a short distance behind a low hill, unaware of the drama taking place nearby.

I hoped, by some stroke of luck, that I was visible to Dave Walter, the Bureau of Land Management field worker who had driven me on to the range. Dave had dropped me from the pickup truck three hours earlier, when I first had spotted the sorrel horse with his mare and colt. I estimated that during that time I had tracked the little band four or five miles and concluded, glumly, that Dave would be too far away to rescue me. In fact, I despaired he would even be able to spot me through his high-powered binoculars.

Deserts are strange places. At first impression a desert is likely to appear flat, although in actuality it may be undulating with many low rises and depressions. Unaccustomed to such an expanse, the eye interprets the vast panorama as level ground, though a camera usually records the topography more faithfully. And so it is possible to walk in the rills of an apparently flat desert and remain hidden. I had deliberately kept low to stalk the horses and now, as a consequence, I was probably obscured from Dave's view.

This was my second field trip to the Kawich Valley in southern Nevada, which is a section of a restricted military reservation, an Air Force practice bombing and gunnery range. On a previous visit I had gained much useful information on the wild horses inhabiting this isolated region. For one thing, I had discovered that they panicked at the mere sight of a pickup truck moving across the horizon. I wondered what military operations might have conditioned the horses to overreact in this way to a far-distant vehicle.

Now on my second visit with permission from the Air Force to remain only over a two-day period when no weapons tests were scheduled, I knew better than to waste precious time in a truck, trying to gain ground on the horses. I would not get within miles of them on wheels. So instead I trekked across the one-hundred-degree desert on foot.

Strange though it may seem, the sight of me walking on the desert did not overly alarm these wild horses. In fact, until I came into close range, my appearance did not even cause them to spook. Quite the contrary, one band stopped to look me over before deciding to move away. I began to suspect that despite their familiarity with man's mechanized trucks, weapons, and planes, human beings in the flesh might be totally unknown to some of these horses. Nevertheless, as I drew near I was careful to move downwind and walk in the depressions. Even with no previous contact with humans, wild animals generally react negatively to our scent. Our odor may possibly be our best natural defense.

Now the gray stallion's glassy-eyed curiosity seemed to give support to my opinion that the animals inhabiting this restricted test site had not had previous contact with people. He gazed at me as if mesmerized and gave his heavy mane a noisy shake. I could hear my heart pounding in my head. In retrospect, I suppose that I, too, may have been somewhat spellbound by his appearance. Never before had I been so close to a wild horse, and he was incredibly beautiful!

As we thus confronted one another the words of a friend echoed in my memory, and I hoped they were not prophetic. I had told him of the profound joy I experience observing wild animals in their natural surroundings, and he had reacted with surprise when he learned that I never carry a gun, and had commented wryly: "Oh well, you'll die happy."

Although, admittedly, in my present predicament, fear, not joy, was my paramount emotion, I still believed that my decision to approach wild horses unarmed was right. For one thing, I have never shared the view of some hunters and journalists who portray the wild stallion as a vicious animal. On the contrary, though he will make a bold stand, his natural defense is his extraordinary speed. And unlike man who has a fragile self-image to protect, a horse is not reluctant to back down and run away if given the opportunity.

However, my reason for not carrying a weapon was not only based on my conviction that most wild horses are harmless; it was also a practical one. My objective was to obtain natural close-up views of the elusive mustangs, and I had noticed before that wild horses often are tolerant of certain harmless species, especially deer and antelope, which they even allow to browse in their midst. And so I decided to gamble that I, too, might gradually be accepted by wild horses if I did not project aggressive signals.

Tracking is only the first of many steps in the tricky process of photographing wild horses. For even though one may succeed in stealing up on a band, the first click of the camera shutter is certain to alert them to the presence of a human being in their habitat and cause them to spook. The end result will be either a quick picture of a startled group of horses looking directly into the camera or a series of photographs of the rear ends of mustangs disappearing into the distance. I soon had a plethora of such pictures, and realized that if I were ever to do better, I must first win a degree of acceptance from the animals so that I could work within a reasonable distance of them over a period of days, or even weeks. It would require more patience than I am usually capable of mustering for ordinary tasks. But photographing wild horses was no ordinary task for me. I can truthfully say that I have never been happier than while tracking mustangs in their wild and beautiful desert and mountain habitats.

Often after moving up on a band, I would spend the next few days doing very little while I let the horses size me up. Not until a particular band showed signs that they were growing accustomed to my presence in their habitat and had begun to resume their normal activities did I attempt to photograph them. In these efforts, failure was the rule. So much depended on how I deported myself the first time I edged into the mustangs' view, and nine-times-out-of-ten, I lost them at this critical point and had to begin all over again, locating, tracking, and winning over another band elsewhere.

I made many mistakes, but I learned from them. For example, I found I could not make too sudden an appearance or I would startle the animals; yet at the same time, I had to be careful not to let the horses see me while I was still a long way off. If they started running while I was still at a distance, they would never learn to identify me. So I tried to sneak up on every band, Indian-style, taking care to move downwind and stay low. When I had managed to get within close range, I gradually revealed my presence by easing into view in the most nonchalant way I could.

Somehow, in that fractional time between the moment when the horses first saw me and the moment when they vanished over a ridge, I had to accomplish two things: . . . arouse their curiosity and communicate my benign attitude. I am convinced that the very act of carrying a gun would have made this very difficult, if not impossible, to do. Animals, being nonverbal, pick up information by observing subtle nuances in one's demeanor. Had I been armed, this would have created in me a more arrogant attitude and changed the very tentative tread of my step into the heavy footfall of the advantaged hunter. I am certain the wild horses would have sensed the difference.

Consequently, I only approached the wild horses on a one-to-one footing; and I viewed any unpleasant experience, such as my present ordeal with the feisty gray stallion, to be a necessary price I must sometimes pay for winning the confidence of mustangs on other occasions.

As the gray horse snorted and took a step toward me, I tried to conjure up positive thoughts about him in order to dispel my fear. I believe that panic reactions often stimulate aggressiveness in an animal. The scream of the rabbit, for example, may actually trigger the hawk to strike the fatal blow. Passivity, not fear, was what I wanted to project.

Suddenly, the gray stallion pulled in his chin until it nearly touched his chest, an action that caused his neck to arch to its full height and his mane to bristle. Then he began to paw in the dust with his front hoofs. I understood the message only too well. He was assuming the display posture of the male horse. I was being invited to do battle!

I dared not make a move lest any action on my part, however slight, be interpreted by the stallion to mean that I, too, was assuming the posture of a male horse in full display and was accepting his challenge.

Although my voice sounded as if it belonged to somebody else, I managed to utter a few soothing words to the gray horse, reserving the loud yell as a final scare tactic should it become necessary. My words, I noted with some encouragement, seemed to have a disarming effect on the wild horse. He raised his head for a moment and regarded me with a a baffled look. Then he blew hard through his nostrils to clear them so that he could better pick up my scent.

Since praise words will evoke a praise tone in the voice of the speaker, I continued to address the horse in endearing terms. Years of talking to my pet dogs apparently have cultivated my ability to communicate my feelings about animals to animals. And on an earlier field trip I had made the surprising discovery that certain wild horses were strangely responsive to my affectionate tone of voice. Later when I described this phenomenon to some ranchers who had had much experience gentling mustangs, they told me that they, too, talked to newly captive wild horses and kept up a steady flow of conversation with the animals throughout their training.

Now the lone gray stallion once again bowed his head and pawed the ground impatiently. I knew that the display is actually a ritualized method by which one stallion measures his dominance against another; each horse showing his muscles, so to speak. And I knew that at any point during the performance of a display, the weaker of the two horses has the option of acknowledging defeat in advance of an actual battle by backing down and running away.

But though I was only too willing to acknowledge defeat in advance, not being another stallion, I did not know how to perform the ritual that would say so, and I was afraid to run away. A wrong movement on my part, I feared, might be construed to be the signal to escalate the fight. So instead I continued to talk. I hoped that my words were carrying the positive ring of my lifelong affection for horses and not the debilitating fear I now was experiencing.

Although on past occasions I had successfully warded off stallion attacks solely through the use of my voice, I could not be sure that the method would always serve me. Every animal is an individual with his own unique reactions that cannot be predicted. Moreover, it occurred to me that I might now be facing a creature who had previously suffered at the hand of man and as a consequence had learned to hate all human beings. At the time, wild horses had no legal protection in America and many were sadly abused. Thousands were gathered in cruel traps or run down by aircraft and trucks and then sold to canneries. Those that escaped grew wary, and a stallion whose mares had been captured by "mustangers" might well attack the next human he encountered.

And this lone gray stallion, though as fit a male as I had ever seen, unaccountably lacked a harem. I wondered why. Lone studs are usually old decrepit animals who have been defeated in battle and lost their harems to stronger males. Most young strong males who have not yet won their harems will run together in stud bands. The gray stallion, obviously, did not fit either of these descriptions. He ran alone, though he was in his prime. As he stood at perfect attention, his two ears held stiffly atop his thick forelock, he emanated health and vigor.

Then suddenly, to my immense relief, he blew a long and contemptuous sounding whinny and bolted off. The sorrel horse had finally spotted him and was rapidly moving his mare and colt away, and the gray shot after them in hot pursuit. Now that I had been released by my captor, it was the sorrel's turn to face the gray, and the contest of wills between the two horses was not likely to end in a truce.

As quick as my fear-numbed arms could manage my equipment, I lifted my camera to my eye and through the lens I watched the sorrel stallion forcing his mare and colt to their utmost speed by running close behind them and wagging his head in the typical herding motion of the wild stallion. Then, as soon as his little band had gained a short lead, he stopped and whirled about to wait for his challenger. His mare and colt, however, continued to run for another five hundred yards before they stopped on the crest of a hill to await the outcome of the inevitable clash that was about to occur between the two males.

In seconds the gray horse caught up to the sorrel stallion and the two horses began to display, arching their necks, posturing, and snorting with gusto. Then a terrible scream burst from the gray stallion and, as if this were a prearranged signal, both animals reared on their hind legs and began to flail the air with their front hoofs. Then, in unison, they lowered themselves to the ground, wheeled, and kicked one another with their powerful hind legs.

The dust they raised was so thick that I could hardly see the action, and I only managed to take one blurry picture before the skirmish was over . . . the sorrel stallion making tracks after his mare and colt, and the defeated gray left standing alone. At that point, I decided to make a swift departure myself before the gray horse decided to return and avenge himself on me.

I may have broken some record for speed-walking that morning. Running from a wild animal is not only futile but risky. It may actually incite an attack. Moreover, even a newborn mustang colt can run faster than the gold-medal winner at the Olympic meets. I have clocked a band of wild horses that contained two very young foals as they ran across painfully rough ground at thirty-five miles an hour.

So without looking back, I simply strode across the desert as rapidly as possible and in less than an hour, I was safely seated in the cab of the pickup truck, rewinding my camera and hoping that I had captured on film one of the most beautiful wild horses I had ever seen.

As it turned out, one black-and-white picture I had taken of the circling gray stallion was used the following year in a nationwide campaign to obtain federal legislation to protect America's dwindling bands of wild horses. More than any other, that photograph became the symbol of the cause of the wild horse. It even graced the front page of *The New York Times* one Sunday morning and illustrated an article that inspired millions of Americans to support a bill granting protection to all such wild, free, and beautiful mustangs as the mysterious lone gray stallion of Kawich Valley.

Stallions

The wild horse is a highly social animal. This fact helps to explain how he came to be domesticated some four thousand years ago. Like the wolf, whose quality of loyal devotion to his own pack made it possible for man to breed him into the dog, the wild horse forms strong bonds with members of his own band. Man had only to exploit this trait and redirect it toward himself in order to make the horse a willing partner in labor, war, and pleasure.

But fidelity and sociability were not, as some have presumed, put into the horse by the Creator for the benefit of man, who could then enslave him. The wolf and the wild horse were both designed to serve their own ends. And though all creatures, including man himself, in some mysterious way appear to serve Nature, the special qualities possessed by the horse and the wolf are attributes that help them to survive.

The social nature of the wild horse is so highly developed that even competitive bands will sometimes form alliances and support each other in time of crisis. But this quality is most clearly seen in his attachment to other members of his own band, which typically consists of a harem of females dominated by a single male. This unit is remarkably stable despite the many outside pressures that threaten it.

Usually a harem numbers from two to eight mares and whatever foals and yearling colts may still be following their mothers. But I have observed larger harems consisting of as many as twenty mares, half of whom had colts, and all of them dominated by one stallion.

Obviously for every stallion that is able to lay claim to twenty mares, there may be nineteen stallions in the vicinity who have no females at all, since an equal number of male and female colts seem to be born. And these unattached males can be a constant source of trouble to the stallion who possesses a harem. Normally, the bachelor studs run together in small all-male bands, and often several members of these bands will act together in an attempt to abduct females. The stallion whose harem is likely to be raided at any hour must, therefore, be constantly on guard against these contenders. As a result, much of his time is spent acting as a sentinel.

Needless to say, the stallion's habit of vigilance is of great importance to his mares and colts, for nothing escapes his attention. And though he may actually be looking for a competitor, at the same time he will not fail to observe any strange sign and will instantly put his mares to flight. A puma, a wolf, or even a photographer, therefore, has a difficult time approaching a band of wild horses. Perhaps it is for this reason that deer and antelope frequently are seen browsing alongside wild horse bands. They may be taking advantage of the stallion's keen alertness to danger.

It is interesting to note, however, that while the stallion seems to be motivated by a jealous interest in safeguarding his territory and his mares from other stallions, he will sometimes grant protection even to his rivals. When lone males or young stud bands are being threatened by predators, a neighboring stallion may temporarily incorporate them into his harem. By some mechanism, intraspecific aggression is inhibited while the male animals unite to fight interspecific forces. I have witnessed several such incidents.

Once, while observing wild horses in the uppermost regions of the Pryor Mountains on the Wyoming-Montana border, I noticed that my presence was particularly unnerving to a pair of old grulla (blue-gray) horses that I called Grandpa and Grandma. Their advanced age was very evident by their sway backs and bony hips, and I doubted that the pair, if faced with a real threat, would be able to make a stand or even run very far. Thus I regarded their nervousness over my daily presence in their habitat to be a realistic response, an accurate assessment of their extreme vulnerability.

One day I decided to move in close to photograph Grandpa and Grandma. I was particularly interested in their relationship, never before having seen an old stud accompanied by an equally ancient mare. Young stallions do not seem to discriminate against aged females; they will add them to their harems with as much zeal as if they were young and beautiful fillies. So I was curious to know how it was that this castaway stallion had managed to hold on to his decrepit female companion.

The mystery was to be compounded. No sooner had I moved within range to photograph the pair than they began to trot back and forth along the crest of the mountain in a fit of anxiety and indecision. To the north lived a tough black stallion with a large harem. For good reason, the grulla male hesitated to head his mare in that direction. To the west lived an unusually large buckskin stallion with an unusually large harem. And to the southeast stood I, armed with lethal-looking cameras.

For a short time the frightened pair was stymied, and while they danced back and forth, I spoke reassuring words to them, hoping they would relax and tolerate a short photographic session. I knew that they had seen me in the area over a period of several days and had probably formed some kind of wild-horse opinion about the degree of threat I represented. I hoped that I had passed muster with them.

But as I clicked away, the pressure on the grulla stallion became too great; he could restrain himself no longer. With his mare in tow he headed across the ridge in a westerly direction, where lived the large buckskin stallion.

The moment the horses topped the ridge, I scrambled up the mountain as fast as I could and managed to scale the top just in time to see the big stallion stalking toward "Gramps" with his neck arched and his chin tucked low. But when the two males came together, a strange thing happened. The buckskin relaxed his display! How and what Gramps had managed to communicate to the powerful male while the two stood calmly facing one another, I will never know; but somehow Grandpa succeeded in making his predicament known. Instead of chasing the intruder back, the brown horse swung around the pair and drove them into his harem!

I managed to get a series of pictures of the two oldsters being herded in the line-up by the big stallion, who intermittently stopped and made fierce stands in my direction. But I felt guilty for having caused this disruption in the lives of Grandpa and Grandma. And I worried that the big dominant stallion would take advantage of the situation, appropriate the old grulla mare, and turn Grandpa away friendless.

To my relief, however, when I returned to the mountaintop the next morning, I found the two old horses back in their usual haunt, their relationship intact. I could only conclude that the buckskin stallion had not been trying to acquire another mare when he had incorporated the alien horses into his harem, but had simply been helping out two vulnerable members of his own species who were being threatened by outside forces.

Not only will a dominant stallion sometimes act to protect a weaker horse, even one of his own sex, but sometimes two or more powerful males will form a liaison and consolidate their harems in order to fight off a common enemy. During the past century, when wolves existed in meaningful numbers and preyed on wild colts, it was not unusual for several wild horse bands to fend off these predators by combining their forces and forming a solid ring around all the foals and yearlings. In this formation, the besieged mustangs would fight long and bitter battles against the hungry wolves who time after time would attempt to penetrate their tightly closed circle. Charles Russell's painting, "Flying Hoofs," dramatically portrays a group of horses defending themselves in this manner. Even to this day, traces of several such conflicts can still be seen etched in the earth.* On a prairie field in northeastern Wyoming, I visited the site of one of these circular battlegrounds where a large number of wild horses once joined together, dug in their rock-hard hoofs and let fly at their attackers.

*The topsoil covering most of the arid Great Plains is extremely thin and easily worn away. Consequently, where heavy abuse by wagon trains, cattle trails, buffalo migratory routes, wild horse battles, or even man's misguided use of the plow has loosened it and caused it to blow away, indelible scars are left on the surface of the earth where plants do not grow for many decades. Even when ground cover finally begins to take root, an indentation remains clearly visible.

As the mating season passes, the intensity of one stallion's antagonism toward another seems to diminish. Some even begin to share common ground. In the fall and winter, many bands abandon their customary ranges and climb to higher altitudes, and it is not unusual to find two stallions who have combined their harems and are co-existing on communal territory over the winter.

Steven W. Pelligrini, who studied wild horses in the Nevada Wassuk Range, observed such a union between two bands for several weeks until it dissolved. He reported that while the individual make-up of the two harems could easily be distinguished when the animals were grazing or resting, during a retreat one of the two stallions invariably demonstrated his dominance over the entire group by running in the superior flank position. When the bands separated late in the winter, however, both harems remained intact. No exchange of mares had taken place.

Inadvertently I have been responsible for inciting several mustang bands to form a single rank simply by trying to approach them in a Land Rover. On the vast, barren Red Desert in southern Wyoming, where untold numbers of mustangs have been pursued and captured by men in trucks and airplanes, the surviving animals are hypersensitive to the approach of any vehicle, and they quickly band together at the mere sound of an engine.

Though this instinctive method of defense worked well against wolves, it has had dire results when used against man. By congregating to protect their weak members, the wild horse bands have frequently helped facilitate their own mass capture. Unfortunately, man's objective, unlike that of the wolf who brought down only the sick, weak, or young animal, has been to round up a whole herd for sale to canneries. As a result, the large bands of wild horses that once graced America's Western mountains, plains, and deserts have rapidly dwindled until today they are bordering on extinction. Such wholesale predation was unforeseen by Nature when she endowed the wild horse with an instinct to come to the defense of young and weak members of his kind.

When wild stallions are not united against a common enemy, they are careful to maintain a respectful distance from one another. For most of the year, each stallion's band inhabits a home range, the boundaries of which appear to overlap to some extent. The border zones are usually treated as joint property by adjacent bands, but when one band penetrates too deeply into the territory of another, the resident stallion immediately puts on such a display of belligerence that the intruders need no further persuasion to retreat.

Pelligrini, in his study of the territoriality and movements of wild horses, discovered that mustang bands, when forced to share a common watering hole, will stagger their visits in an apparent effort to avoid encounters. If one band arrives before another has finished watering, it awaits its turn at a polite distance. Thus it appears that the wild horse's biotype not only may be affected by a space plan but also by a time plan.

Pelligrini reported, however, that a very dominant stallion would interrupt any horses he found at the spring and force them to leave and wait until his band had finished watering.

My own observations have convinced me that Pelligrini is correct in suggesting there may be a pecking order among some wild horse bands using a particular region. Over a three-year period I made numerous field trips to study the wild horses that inhabit a long corridor at the base of the Pryor Mountains. Locally, the long strip of land is referred to as Sykes Valley for a colorful nineteenth-century homesteader (said to have had two Indian wives) whose abandoned shack still stands there. During my many visits, I observed that the horses in the region gave wide berth to one dark mahogany stallion that I, inappropriately, named the Black King when I first saw him in dim light. The Black King and his large harem of mares and colts occupied roughly 50 per cent of the vast area, though they numbered fewer than 20 per cent of the horses living there.

The first time I observed the Black King, he possessed a harem of fourteen mares and seven colts, the largest in the entire Pryor Mountain Range. The following year, when I visited the area again, I counted three fewer mares in the Black King's harem, but as I did not find them in neighboring harems, I doubt they were captured by other stallions, but suspect they had died over the winter.

On the other hand, the three missing mares may have been the grown daughters of the Black King, in which case it is likely that he evicted them himself. Contrary to common belief, wild horses generally do not inbreed. Robert Brislawn, who for decades has observed mustangs that run wild on his private lands in northeastern Wyoming, reports that stallions expel their fillies at an earlier age than they oust their stud colts. When a female offspring comes into her first heat, her sire will drive her off his range. Naturally, while in this condition, the filly will be quickly picked up by a neighboring stallion and added to his harem. Thus, some exchange of females appears to take place without conflict between males.

But by whatever means the Black King's harem had been reduced to eleven mares, it still exceeded the next largest in the region by three. It was also unique in another respect. The Black King, it seemed, had a predilection for mares of a particular color and had surrounded himself with a bevy of brunettes. Although some two hundred wild horses inhabiting the Pryor Mountain range are renowned for their varied colors, the harem of the Black King contained only reddish-brown mares with black manes and tails, commonly known as bays. The only exception was a reddish-brown sorrel mare whose mane and tail matched her body. However, the sorrel's body was the same shade as the bays'. No grays, grullas, roans, buckskins, blacks, or palominos graced the Black King's domain, although these were the colors that predominated in adjacent bands.

I could only speculate on the difficulty he must have had in assembling such a harem. Perhaps after every victory in battle with another male, the Black King singled out only one mare whose color was to his liking, leaving the others to his defeated opponent; and so, little by little, he acquired this large and extraordinary collection of females.

Although it is a fact that horses do not see color as we do, they are able to distinguish lighter shades from darker ones. It is possible, therefore, that Black King had a preference for the deeper tones of the red-brown hue over the paler shades of yellow buckskin and blue grulla so prevalent in the area. Or perhaps some other quality in the mares, by chance, happened to be genetically linked to the red-brown color, and it was actually this trait to which the Black King responded.

On the other hand, we know little of what horses actually see through their wide-set eyes. Not only is their angle of vision very different from our own, but their ability to see at night suggests the possibility, at least, that they may visualize wave lengths beyond our range. We cannot imagine how a red-brown mare appears to a wild stallion!

Whatever the explanation, I have observed several instances in which a stallion seemed to show a preference for mares of a particular shade. If, as some people have suggested, a solid-colored harem could be explained as being the end product of incestuous breeding, the "sire" might be expected to match the females. But in only one instance was this true. Usually the stallion has been a different color than his mares, indicating they are not his offspring.*

While working in Sykes Valley, my photographic efforts naturally centered on the bands that could learn to tolerate my presence to some degree. But even these would spook if I failed to maintain a respectful distance. On occasion, when I, inadvertently, approached too close, I sometimes caused a band to leave its home range and move on to alien territory. Yet only once, under unusual circumstances, did a band cross into the vast domain occupied by the Black King, although he made frequent solo sorties into the range of his neighbors.

The Black King, for all his aggressiveness, will always remain my favorite mustang. He was a common-looking horse with no outstanding feature to commend him. Yet he seemed so completely in command of himself at all times I never grew tired of watching him. Moreover, he was the fastest mustang I have ever seen. Once, when I went to the races I bet on every horse that vaguely resembled him and, to my surprise, found I had picked a win, place, or show ticket in every race!

Though it is the nature of the male horse to be possessive of his females, the Black King seemed to overdo it. He behaved like a domineering tyrant, lording it over his harem, gathering and herding the mares and tightening their ranks, sometimes for no apparent purpose. This instinctive herding behavior on the part of the stallion is normal and is probably an important survival factor, for it keeps the band unified and compact. A scattered harem is at a disadvantage in a crisis. Any horse that is separated from the others, even by a short distance, is likely to be singled out as the prey of a wolf, a puma, or even a human "mustanger."

The zealous Black King never allowed the members of his harem to become dispersed.

*One of the Black King's colts was dark mahogany like himself and that animal, a filly, was absent from his band the following year.

When any mare grazed too far from the others, he either moved his entire band to join her or he approached the meanderer with outstretched neck, his head lowered and weaving like a snake under the hypnotic influence of music, and herded her back into the ranks.

The grotesque herding posture of the wild stallion is an expedient and valuable signal that substitutes for more forceful behavior. A stray mare clearly comprehends the meaning of an outstretched neck and a wagging head; by complying and permitting herself to be herded about by the stallion, she can avoid being nipped. The stallion uses this display to start a retreat, to tighten the harem's ranks, and to force his mares to a faster pace when pursued by an enemy. In short, it is one nonviolent means by which the wild stallion can control the members of his band.

On more than one occasion I have watched the Black King assume this herding posture and drive his mares back and forth across the length of Sykes Valley in what appeared to be no more than a drill. The mares, running single file as is their habit, rushed frantically from one end of the canyon floor to the other for more than a half-hour. They were not being pursued nor were they going any place; yet the stallion relentlessly drove them on at top speed, and whenever the line began to flag, he nipped the unfortunate mare who ran just ahead of him.

The Black King may only have been letting off some of his superabundant energy that evening, but, whatever motivated him, his mares and colts were well exercised by the maneuver, and after a day of quiet grazing, they may even have enjoyed the activity. Such a workout, if performed regularly, would have the positive value of keeping the band in top running form.

Regardless of how capricious a stallion may be in selecting females, or how overbearing might be his conduct toward the ones he finally gathers, his ultimate allegiance to them is the stuff from which many legends have been spun. Though many of the tales may be exaggerated, the stallion's loyalty to his mares is indeed impressive and cannot be explained by sexual attraction alone. Unlike buck deer and bull elk, both of whom gather females only when the does and cows are in season, the male mustang retains his harem the year round, despite the fact that wild mares come into heat only in the spring and early summer, one month after giving birth.*

Although domestic mares as a group are irregular in this respect, some coming into heat even in the fall and winter, all wild mares come into season some time between April and July. Perhaps this cycle has evolved through natural selection. A foal born too late would not be sufficiently nourished before the onset of winter, and with feed scarce and temperatures low, the nursing mother would have no better chance of surviving the cold months than would her unweaned offspring. Both would be eliminated by natural forces.

*The gestation period of the mare is eleven months, and she comes into heat one month after foaling. Consequently, if a mare is mated annually, she will foal in the same month every year.

The wild stallion's loyalty to his mares is to some extent extended also to his colts, but individual stallions differ greatly in their degree of involvement with their offspring. Whereas mares enjoy lifetime status in the band (or at least until the stallion grows too old to defend them), colts are accepted only until they reach maturity. Sometimes, in the case of males, this may be for as long as three years, or until the young studs become aggressive and begin to squeal.

I once saw the Black King retrieve one of his colts who had accidentally joined a strange harem during an encounter between the two bands on the periphery of his own territory. The colt had taken off with the alien mares while the Black King and the "invading" stallion were confronting each other. The "trespasser" gamely faced the Black King while his harem escaped, then he bowed to the Black King's dominance and accepted the option of the display ritual which permitted him to back down and run away.

But the victorious Black King, after returning to his own waiting harem, suddenly missed his offspring, whereupon he streaked after the fleeing band and overtook it. As I watched the big horse single out his own and begin to drive the renegade colt to home range, I held my breath for fear the foal would be trampled to death by the impatient stallion who put on such a burst of speed the little fellow was pushed to his limit. As the Black King pressed the young defector homeward, he so exaggerated his herding posture, stretched his neck so absurdly and carried his head so low to the ground he resembled an angry goose. Fortunately, the colt, having been sired by the tough stallion, had inherited the stamina to keep the pace and managed to reach the safety of his mother's side.

Though the Black King never hesitated to enter the ranges of his neighbors to retrieve a colt or to exercise his mares (if that, in fact, is what he was doing), no horses trespassed on his territory. One day, however, I spotted a stray cow and calf in the area and watched as they headed onto the domain of the Black King.

Seemingly oblivious to the mustangs' presence, the bovine mother, with her calf at her heels, boldly cut through the startled harem of the Black King and, without shifting her gaze or her direction, trudged past the surprised stallion, himself, as if he were nonexistent. But though she put up a bold front, she revealed her anxiety by bellowing like a ship in distress throughout her resolute march. The Black King watched the outrageous performance with an expression of helpless perplexity, looking for all the world like a stuffy gentleman who is embarrassed by the antics of a lady, but who has no notion on earth of how to cope with her.

I noted the brands on the stray cattle and that night notified the rancher who owned them. He told me he had lost them many miles away during a cattle drive, and seemed delighted they had been located. The next day when he and his wife and daughter arrived on horseback to round them up, I pointed out the Black King to them and described some of his ways. The rancher was so intrigued by my story and so eager to be helpful to my project he immediately proposed a plan whereby he and his wife and daughter would ride across the valley, surround a band of mustangs, and drive them on to the range of the dominant stallion. All I would have to do would be to sit tight and wait for the inevitable hostilities that would arise between the two male horses. According to the rancher, I was certain to get some outstanding photographs of a stallion fight.

I opposed the plan on principle, explaining that I did not want to disrupt the normal lives of the wild horses any more than I already had by my presence in the area. But the rancher, a determined sort of Westerner when it came to helping a friend, could not be dissuaded. While I sat on a hill, the three riders galloped off in the direction of a band of six mustangs. Being expert cowpunchers, they had little difficulty slipping around the mustangs, and they soon had triggered a stampede that carried the little band halfway across the long valley. Nevertheless, only by pushing their cow ponies (descendants of mustangs) to the limit were they able to keep pace with the fleet-footed wild horses and hold positions on three sides of the panicked band.

Despite my qualms as the six mustangs headed toward the territory of the Black King at breakneck speed, I could not help but be interested in the outcome. As the pounding of hoofbeats grew louder, my own excitement mounted.

Suddenly, I heard the Black King scream and I looked around to see the sovereign horse trotting stiffly and with great dignity toward the charging animals. As he neared his boundary, he stepped up his pace and tipped his head in readiness for the preliminary display that precedes or substitutes for battle. His mares, at a signal from him, had already lined up and were in retreat, led by his only distinguishable female, the one whose mane and tail matched her red-brown body.

I raised my camera to my eye, anticipating the showdown, when suddenly the stampeding horses swerved, and like a quadrille of dancers, slipped through the riders and began to backtrack to their home range at top speed. By the time the riders realized what had happened and had turned their mounts, the mustangs were already a long way off.

Afterward, the rancher, who had been a mustang-watcher all his life, expressed astonishment that the six wild horses had chosen to run through human ranks rather than risk an encounter with the Black King. And he expressed even more surprise that the Black King, instead of spooking at the sight of the advancing cavalcade of wild horses and yelling riders, had defiantly come forward to meet them.

But I was not surprised. I had spent hundreds of hours watching the Black King and I would have put my money on him in any heat or handicap devised by man.

25

Young Stud Bands

When I first encountered the Juvenile Delinquents in 1970, they were about four years old. Though the two young males were not the same color, their markings were so much alike that I suspected they were half brothers, sired by the same father out of two different mares in his harem. Both had bald faces, or, as a Westerner might put it, white blazes so long that they swallowed them. And both wore matched socks on their hind feet. But the golden sorrel was slightly smaller and more delicately built than his black companion.

After watching these two rambunctious troublemakers in action in Sykes Valley, I began to call them the Juvenile Delinquents, or the J.D.s for short. The pair showed no respect for any order imposed on the area by the harem-possessing stallions who resided there. Whatever boundaries and home ranges had gradually been established in the valley through protracted tests of male strength (whether in actual battles or by mere symbolic display), these were totally disregarded by the two adolescent horses who roamed at will across the vast area, poaching grass here, teasing a stallion into chasing them there, and in general creating confusion and disorder.

Like all males their age, they exuded energy and aggression, but were still too young and inexperienced to gather and defend females. The first year I met them, they were probably still cutting permanent teeth.

It is not strange that the J.D.s should have paired off together. It is natural for a young male, after being ousted from his parental band, to seek companionship with another in the same plight. The horse is a social animal and does not like to run alone. So young outcasts "gang up" and, for a few years, while they are maturing and developing their fighting skills, they roam widely and prevent the established stallions in the region from becoming too complacent.

It was clear to me that the Juvenile Delinquents were as delighted with their life-style as they were with one another's company. Their relationship demonstrated the strong *bond-behavior* that is so characteristic of horses; they were inseparable.

Even domestic horses, whose survival hardly depends on cooperation among themselves, often choose individual friends from among their own species. Many a Thoroughbred, for example, requires that a particular horse from the home stable accompany him while he is touring the race-track circuit; and if, for some reason, he is separated from his side-kick, he does poorly on the track. Like dogs and people, horses form strong individual attachments.

The friendship of the J.D.s epitomized this bonding between two horses. They watered and rolled and grazed and fought side by side. And when they relaxed, they stood head-to-tail and flicked flies off one another's face with their long, thick tails. Or one groomed the other by gently nibbling cockleburs out of his unkempt mane.

From the first day I came upon the J.D.s grazing in a patch of yellow wild flowers, I was charmed by them, and I resolved to spend the remainder of that particular field trip following their trail. At the time I lacked good close-up pictures of a stallion fight, and I counted on this pair to stir up trouble for me so that I could photograph a battle.

Though I had witnessed numerous conflicts, my pictures had always been disappointing. Either I had not moved in rapidly enough before the stallions had settled their dispute, or the horses had fought on the run and I could not keep up with them. In many cases, when I heard a male war cry and raced to the source of the commotion, my very appearance caused the combatants to break off. Furthermore, it became apparent to me that most conflicts do not escalate beyond the display stage. The animals in the region were well acquainted with one another and had settled questions of mares, ranges, and dominance long before I began observing them. An arched neck and a snort was usually all that was needed to remind a less dominant animal of an ignominious past defeat, and he would back down and run away. Nature did not design the wild horse to be so pugnacious that he would exterminate himself.

But the Juvenile Delinquents had not yet tested their male prowess and they looked for opportunities to do so. Moreover, they were vagabonds, claiming no home range; therefore, they were at all times on dangerous ground since the entire area was apportioned among the males with harems. As a result, whenever the two interlopers were spotted by the resident stallion upon whose range they happened to be poaching, action quickly developed.

For these reasons, the young horses were catalysts of trouble, and they fought like trained guerrillas. Generally, they stationed themselves about twenty feet apart on opposite sides of a displaying stallion and while one distracted him by snorting loudly and posturing in an exaggerated manner, the other member of the pair attacked. When the ambushed stallion recovered from the shock and turned to face his young assailant, the first Juvenile Delinquent would hit him from the other side. In the end, however, the J.D.s were compelled to concede every battle. They were not yet capable of defeating an older male, and so they blithely abandoned every fight they instigated and danced off in search of new adventures.

During my first field trip to Sykes Valley, the two horses probably were still too young to retain any spoils, had they been able to vanquish their opponent. For victory would not only have required them to settle onto home ranges, but would have committed them to the defense of harems. And the J.D.s were still sowing their wild oats. Few wild stallions in fact gather females much before they are six or seven years old.

Although one or both of the young horses often appeared to receive heavy clouts when a stallion's hind hoof resounded sharply on a rib or jaw, neither ever seemed to incur serious injuries. Once, however, after a particularly rough skirmish in which the golden sorrel received several brutal blows, the pair retired to a sheltered meadow and consoled one another for the remainder of the afternoon. Heads resting upon withers and glassy-eyed, each gave the other solace in a quiet exchange understood only by horses and by a few people who have watched horses over a long period of time.

Finally, though, a day did arrive when I came upon the Juvenile Delinquents in possession of a mare. I did not witness how they had gained their prize, so I will never know whether she, like themselves, had been expelled from a parental band by her sire and thus had been easy pickings for the pair, or if they had taken her away from another male in one of their storm-trooper actions which, heretofore, had always ended in their own defeat. One afternoon, however, after having searched for them for nearly a whole day, I finally stumbled across the young horses in an out-of-the-way valley, and lo! standing between them was as young and lovely a bay filly as I had seen in a long time.

Now, thought I, this female will split up a beautiful friendship. The Juvenile Delinquents' salad days have finally come to an end. The situation was loaded with dramatic possibilities, and I rejoiced over my good fortune in chancing upon so unusual a development. But my four-week field trip was about to end. I was leaving in two days, and I feared the J.D.s might not resolve this new complication in so short a period.

However, action began almost immediately. A band of horses that habitually watered each evening at sunset was slowly easing down the mountain en route to a creek that bisected the valley. As I watched them wend their way through the mountain mahogany brush, I suddenly remembered that their normal route of travel would carry them directly into the place where the Juvenile Delinquents had secluded their newly acquired female. I waited with excrutiating anticipation. Although I badly wanted pictures of a stallion fight, I feared for the J.D.s' safety. With such high stakes—a female in heat!—the fight I was certain I was about to witness was unlikely to be conceded easily.

I did not have to wait long. The approaching stallion, a bay, must have picked up the scent of the young filly, for he suddenly galloped past his drifting harem and headed in a straight line

29

for the trio of horses. At thirty feet he paused on the crest of a hill and arrogantly surveyed the scene.

Exactly at that moment, the black J.D. could hardly have been at more of a disadvantage. He was mating with the young female! But his friend, the golden sorrel, rose to the occasion and, alone, rushed forward to meet the intruder. Valiantly, he took on the older horse and, despite the fact that the smaller J.D. was unaccustomed to fighting without the aid of his partner, he actually succeeded in routing the stallion from the valley.

Then an interesting thing happened. After a short interval, the sorrel J.D. took his turn with the filly while the black horse stood guard and watched for the approach of a rival. And so, over the remainder of the afternoon, the two horses spelled one another; while one mated the other stood guard.

Before it grew dark another stallion did arrive to investigate, alerted no doubt to the situation by a gusty wind. At that moment, however, it was the sorrel J.D. who was incapacitated and the black J.D. who interposed and drove the contender away with a bravado, previously not evident in his nature. Since neither of the J.D.s had ever been capable of holding his own in battle, I could only attribute the instant and remarkable improvement in their fighting skills to the sudden appearance of a female in their lives.

I studied the young filly closely and tried to recall if I had ever seen her before. As she was a bay, I decided to visit the Black King's band the following morning to make a count of his females: I did and none were missing.

Unlike the J.D.s, the filly did not seem to be a willing participant in this newly formed *ménage à trois*. On several occasions she kicked one or both of the J.D.s and they responded unchivalrously by kicking her back. From a purely personal viewpoint, I was upset by their behavior and worried about the young filly. I hardly knew whether to regard her as the unfortunate captive of two ruffians, or to see her as the only female wild horse who not only did not have to share her mate with a harem of other females, but whose happy fate it was to have two suitors dancing attendance on her. For once, at least, the typical polygamous roles of the wild mare and stallion had been reversed.

But whatever aversion the filly demonstrated that evening, the following day all three animals appeared to be as happy as young foals; they even stood in a tight three-way huddle to shield one another's bodies from flies. The female now made no further attempt to escape from her captors and the J.D.s still showed no signs of jealousy.

It occurred to me that I might be witnessing a fairly normal behavior pattern, albeit one that had previously gone unnoticed. Perhaps it is not uncommon for a stud band to serve as the nucleus for the formation of a new harem. Possibly young studs with long-standing ties continue to coexist for a period of time while they acquire females.

I began to ponder this hypothesis. Several males acting together obviously would stand a better chance of making a successful raid for females than would a lone horse. I had often wondered how a single and inexperienced male ever managed to assemble a harem. Bearing in mind that the mares, the object of a young stallion's offensive, often disappear over a ridge while he is attacking their mate, one begins to see the difficulties involved.

Moreover, even if the challenger is able to put up a respectable fight while on the periphery of the resident stallion's territory, he will very likely be defeated if he tries to pursue the mares into the heart of their home range. Konrad Lorenz in his book *On Aggression* has pointed out that an animal is most proficient at defending the center of his own range where his familiarity with his surroundings enhances his readiness to fight. By contrast, the deeper an interloper penetrates alien ground, the less "safe" he feels and the more easily he will be intimidated. At a certain point, his readiness to fight is replaced by an instinctive impulse to take flight.

I had certainly noticed this behavior in conflicts between wild stallions. But by working together, a band of young studs could overcome this handicap; one horse could head off a mare while his partner fended off her mate. Actually, I had seen this strategy tried by stud bands on many occasions, but the question of what would happen next, should their tactic succeed, had somehow not occurred to me before. Perhaps, even after several females have been captured, the "charter members" of the stud band remain too closely bonded to sever relations with one another immediately. For a period of time, the band may simply be enlarged to include both male and female members. I remember seeing one such band in southern Nevada, and I recalled that Pelligrini had mentioned sighting several bands comprised of both sexes in the Wassuk Range.

If my theory proved correct, the J.D.s might well remain allies for some time to come while they continued to capture a number of females. Eventually, however, a day of reckoning would arrive when their fraternal attachments would break down, not over the females, whom the two males would by then be accustomed to sharing, but in contests over rank.

Unfortunately, I could not stay to witness the final rupture between the two J.D.s. When I left Sykes Valley, the three horses were still living amicably together. However, when I returned sixteen months later, I found the black J.D. not only still in possession of the female but, in the tradition of the Black King, he had added two more bay mares to his entourage. The golden sorrel, on the other hand, was nowhere to be found. I never saw him again.

This hypothesis helped to explain a drama I had photographed in southern Nevada the previous year. The incident took place in the Kawich Range, where, one fine day, I came upon a band of horses that contained two mature stallions, a gray and a black. It was obvious from the stallions' behavior that both were equally at home among the females, as well as on the territory; all the horses grazed peacefully together. Yet, whenever, either stallion approached too near the other, both began to strut and squeal. I hid and watched.

For a time, no action developed; the two male horses merely circled and stayed out of each other's way. Then the band formed a line and began to move off. But instead of only one male occupying the dominant flank position, both stallions claimed it and ran side by side as if in tandem.

This so aggravated the two of them that they soon stopped and began to perform an elaborate display ritual. Pressing their foreheads together, they eyeballed one another for what seemed an interminable length of time, looking for all the world like two antlered animals whose horns had locked. Then suddenly, the black broke away, whereupon the mares again lined up, and for the second time the band began to move. Now, however, only one horse, the victorious gray, occupied the flank position.

But if the gray thought he had banished his rival, he was mistaken, for the black had merely galloped to the front of the line and usurped the place of the lead-mare, whose status in the hierarchy of the band is second only to that of the stallion. For a short while the animals proceeded, led by the black and flanked by the gray. Then, suddenly the gray spotted the black stallion at the head of the line, and, in a burst of speed, he overtook the female impersonator.

Once again the black and gray confronted one another. But as before, their conflict was more sound and fury than action. Though they protested noisily, they swatted one another only lightly as each bid for a bloodless victory. This time, however, it was the black stallion who outbluffed the gray and who consummated his victory by taking the coveted end position.

But though the gray appeared to back off, he no more had conceded this battle than the black had conceded the earlier one. His stratagem was to join the harem, running in an insignificant position within the female ranks. For a time this arrangement seemed to mollify the black stallion, and I had the strong impression that he would tolerate the continuing presence of the gray provided he would remain in this subordinate place.

But soon the gray stallion made a new bid for the dominant spot. Little by little, he began to fall back in the line-up until once again he and the black were running side by side. Again the band halted as the two males, for the third time, repeated their ritualized confrontation.

Finally, I could remain concealed no longer while at the same time keeping pace with the moving horses. As I dashed across a low hill, one of them spotted me and, within seconds, the band had vanished, their dust merging with the shimmering haze that edged the desert horizon.

Though I did not learn the outcome, that conflict raised many questions in my mind. At the time, I ascribed the bizarre performance of the two males to filial rebellion. A stallion perhaps was trying to drive an insurgent son from his band; the offspring was resisting being expelled and challenging the sire for control of the harem. But now, in retrospect, it seems equally plausible that I had witnessed the day of reckoning between two young stallions who together had gathered the harem.

In either case, it was clear to me that the two horses had previously enjoyed some type of tie that was finally breaking down. It also seemed clear that the rivalry slowly building up between them was only indirectly related to the females. Each male appeared willing to tolerate the other one, even among the mares, providing he remain in a subordinate position in the line-up. The aim of each was to gain and hold the dominant spot in the band. Inevitably, if their conflict continued to escalate, one or the other would be driven away and the victor would remain the sole stallion in charge of the harem. Thereafter, with all male bonds severed, no strange stallion would be allowed to approach.

My theory will remain only a theory until long-range studies have been made, but I am convinced of one thing: the mature stallion's drive to be dominant is exceedingly strong and in certain respects may outweigh his sex drive. He herds females the year round, despite the fact that their mating season is very short. His faithful association with them cannot be attributed to sex drive alone and may, in large part, be motivated by his very strong inclination to dominate other horses. He might as happily herd passive males with whom he has formed bonds as his band of submissive females were it not for the fact that passive males sooner or later begin to develop the same drive to be dominant. At that point conflict arises, and whether the males be father and son or friends from an adolescent stud band, all previous bonds dissolve when the two stallions begin to compete for dominance. Finally one of them must leave.

More Stud Bands

Another band of young males also inhabited Sykes Valley. I named this foursome the Banditos, for besides being outlaws, they closely resembled the fiery mounts of the sixteenth-century conquistadores that were to become the seed stock for the vast population of wild horses that exploded across the West more than three centuries ago. I felt certain that the Banditos still carried some Spanish Barb blood.

Two members of this juvenile gang hardly looked to be more than yearlings. Both were bays—one a sandy shade; the other, reddish-brown like many of the Black King's progeny. As later events indicated, the latter may have been one of the Black King's ousted sons.

A third Bandito was approximately four years old; a shiny black beauty with one white sock on his near hind foot and a crooked blaze that trickled down his face like spilled milk. I called this handsome firebrand Blackie.

The fourth member, Buck, was a Roman-nosed buckskin with a number of black rings encircling each leg like bracelets, a wide stripe down his back, and another one across his shoulders. Striping in wild horses is believed to be a reversion to the most primitive horse marking. Zebras, wild asses (or onagers), and even Przhevalski's wild horse, all bear stripes in varying degrees. So when stripes begin to show up in a wild horse herd, many knowledgeable people regard it as proof that the animals are descended from many long generations of wild mustangs.

I rarely saw the Banditos during the daytime and I never did discover where they hid out. Probably, when they were not loping about the old Sykes homestead site, they were making their presence felt higher up in the Pryor Mountain range. At any rate, each afternoon, when the sun's rays began to angle obliquely into the valley, bathing the sage and cottonwoods in yellow light, the four Banditos would appear, prancing and snorting.

I loved to watch as they stalked across the wide valley. Buck and Blackie frequently would travel a fair distance in full display. They were terrible show-offs. And they nearly always permitted me to obtain a good view of their antics. I had invested no small amount of time wooing them with endearing words, even with songs, and, as a result, all four had grown accustomed to my presence.

Once, however, while working at unusually close range, I made a near-fatal mistake. I had just shot the last picture on my film and while seated on the ground reloading my camera, I failed to notice the effect my change in posture had produced on the Banditos. Suddenly, a rustle in the grass alerted me, and I glanced up just in time to see Buck, with his ears laid back, charging me head-on.

Instantly, I sprang to my feet, and the shriek that I let out stopped him neatly in his tracks. During the next thirty seconds the verbal barrage that poured out of me really appeared to discomfit Buck, who previously had heard nothing but blandishments from me. For a few moments he studied me with a puzzled expression, then he turned on his heels and was gone.

I don't know whether he had momentarily mistaken me for a coyote lurking in the grass, or perhaps he had thought I was a mountain lion, crouched and ready to pounce, but ever after I was careful to remain on my two legs and plainly identifiable when in the presence of the Banditos. It was a valuable lesson and a reminder to me that I was dealing with wild, not tame horses.

The two older Banditos, Buck and Blackie, were almost never quiet. When not engaged in mock battle, they raced wildly about the valley, making sudden stops from time to time to perform magnificent displays. They even played at herding. Both vied to dominate the all-male band, and after every skirmish, each would assume the grotesque herding posture of the mature wild stallion and try to drive the other where he pleased. Failing this, the two would then focus attention on their younger companions and bully and herd them about.

I was fascinated to see how these bachelor males practiced the behavior they would someday employ to control and defend harems. I was also fascinated to see that only Buck and Blackie actually engaged in mock combat. The younger males not only refrained from all aggressive play, but, in the manner of females, passively allowed themselves to be driven and herded by the stronger and more dominant males. As far as the two younger Banditos were concerned, some kind of pecking order seemed to have been rigidly established.

Not so with Buck and Blackie. Whenever Blackie tried to herd Buck, or Buck tried to herd Blackie, a sparring match would erupt. And though the fight might be a sham, the moment the mock battle ended, the combatant who thought he had subdued the other would once again try to herd him. I viewed their behavior as strong evidence that the physical posture of harem-herding is the means by which a wild stallion confirms his dominance. I concluded that the male horse probably remains with his females the year round, despite the fact that they represent infrequent sexual satisfaction, because they allow him to satisfy this equally basic drive for dominance.

One evening while trailing behind the Banditos, I noted with some apprehension that the band was nearing the territory of the Black King. As they moved across the valley single file, engaging as usual in high-spirited play, Buck or Blackie made frequent stops to let out a long whinny that seemed to say, "Here I am, I'm alive!" and the other three would wait while the horse making the declaration would punctuate it by rearing on his hind legs and pawing the air with his forefeet.

I believe I saw the Black King before they did. Like the Assyrians of old, the mahogany stallion charged down the slope like a wolf on a fold, and the four-against-one battle which I realized was about to erupt looked to me to be an even match.

The melee that followed is still not entirely clear in my mind. I recall a swirl of horses, kicking and roaring and moving. I recall being at one time in the center of the action and springing from side to side faster than my mind could think. But wherever I leaped, the horses were pounding toward me, circling, whirling, clouting one another with savage kicks, tearing at manes, and screaming.

Though there was no time to focus my camera, I clicked away haphazardly, while side-stepping and dodging the five-way free-for-all that raged about me. It was like trying to work in the middle of an erratic tornado.

One picture I hardly remember taking at the time was published by the *National Geographic Magazine* and captioned: "Double uppercut stuns stallion." It was Buck's one moment of glory when he caught the Black King under the chin with both hind feet. Luckily, it was in perfect focus!

Then, although I missed seeing how it happened, the little bay yearling was on the ground, and the Black King had his mane in his teeth and was ripping it out. With each yank, tufts of black horsehair came out and hung like a scalp trophy from the stallion's mouth. To my horror, the victim's cohorts did not come to his rescue. Instead, like a pack of canines turning on an underdog, they, too, began to tear at the little bay's mane.

I regarded this perfidious behavior of the Banditos as ostensible proof that wild horses organize themselves into dominance-subordination relationships that are extremely complex. Turncoat behavior is typical of species that observe a "peck-order." In such animal societies when one member of the hierarchy is forced by another to cry "uncle," bystanders very often will jump into the fray to affirm their own superior rank to the victim. However, it rarely follows that the low-ranking victim is destroyed by the individuals who mob him. In fact, his very submissiveness makes it all but impossible for his attackers to seriously injure him, and their "peck" finally becomes ritualized into a virtually harmless gesture.

Just so with the Black King and the Banditos. Though the low-ranking bay yearling was down on the ground in a perilously vulnerable position, his attackers were not actually drawing blood. In fact, hair-pulling appeared to have become a symbolic substitute for real biting! Not only had the bay's passivity saved him, but it had served to dampen the riotous expression of raw aggression that only seconds before had been raging around me. I was amazed to see such a clear demonstration of the peck-order principle which holds that by maintaining a submissive posture, a defeated animal can inhibit further aggression in his attacker. Upon reflection, however, I realized that I, myself, instinctively display passivity whenever I am menaced by wild stallions. Some part of me has always known about this.

But though the young bay suffered no mutilation, what humiliation he endured! Even after he had struggled to his feet, he continued to submit to the indignity of having his mane pulled by four horses, and when at last they had finished with him he was a sorry sight. With his head hanging low and his mane in tatters, he managed to drag himself a few yards away, where he stood in such a dejected posture he looked a hundred years old. Though my heart went out to him I was, nevertheless, pleased that the fighting code of the wild horse had operated to prevent real physical damage from being inflicted on this perfectly able-bodied though less stalwart member of the species who had acknowledged his low rank.

Then round two erupted. This proved to be a four-way brawl with the defeated bay yearling counted out. He seemed sunk in a catatonic stupor, and as the contest swirled around him, appeared to take no notice. The Black King, however, had no difficulty recovering his aggressive spirit. It took him less than a minute to rout the three Banditos and send them flying over a rise. As the three horses disappeared from view, leaving their fellow Bandito behind them, the wilderness suddenly became tranquil again. Only raised dust marked the spot where seconds before the violent struggle had taken place.

The triumphant Black King pursued the fleeing Banditos a short distance and then turned back and headed toward the young male who remained near me in a trancelike state, as if awaiting a sentence. And, indeed, a most unusual sentence was imposed on him. To my astonishment, the Black King swung round the lowly Bandito and herded him like a female to his harem of mares grazing some yards away, apparently oblivious to the conflict that had raged about them.

Needless to say, I had never before seen one stallion capture another, and I had difficulty making any sense out of the behavior. One idea, however, struck me as a plausible explanation. I theorized that the bay male could actually have been the Black King's recently expelled offspring. If such were the case, previous bonds between the two horses might have been reactivated after the yearling exhibited so much abject submissiveness.

Actually, since it was unusual for any horse as young as this bay to be already separated from his parental band, I wondered if he had perhaps inherited the Black King's aggressive disposition and, as a consequence, forced a too early rupture between his sire and himself. If so, life in the stud band had certainly deflated him; he was no match for Buck or Blackie.

Moreover, after being mobbed by four horses, he was further humbled, and his present demeanor presented no challenge to the Black King's supremacy.

For his part, the Black King seemed totally contented with his battle spoils, and he herded the passive young stallion into his harem of females with as much alacrity as if he had just gained another mare.

But the strange story did not end there. Buck, after recovering his composure a safe distance away, apparently missed the young companion he had grown so accustomed to bullying, and he made a daring attempt to recapture him. Unaccompanied by the other Banditos, he galloped the entire length of the valley and managed to swing round to the back of the Black King's harem before the mighty monarch again spotted him.

The chase that followed told me everything there was to know about Black King. He rocketed down the length of the valley like some kind of jet-propelled missile, pouring on fuel as he traveled. Poor Buck ran the race of his life, with the Black King gaining on him every stride of the way. Every few minutes I could see the tired buckskin exerting a supreme effort to surge a little ahead, only to flag again and lose more ground. He would not have lasted and would have shortly been overtaken but for the fact that the Black King lost interest in pursuing him and turned and galloped the two or more miles back to his band.

Though both Buck and I were exhausted from our part in the ordeal, the Black King did not show the slightest sign of fatigue. In fact, upon returning to his home range, he decided it was high time for a drill and he rounded up all the members of his now slightly enlarged band and herded them from one end of the valley to the other.

Never, but never, was there a horse like the Black King!

Mares and Colts

One day while looking for wild horses in a remote section of the Pryor Mountains, I almost walked past a newborn colt without noticing him. Where the foal lay, curled in the brush like a desert bud, he was well camouflaged. His mother had hidden him carefully and gone off to graze or to water.

I expected I would soon find her, not too far distant and by herself, it being the habit of wild mares to go off alone to give birth. If this colt's mother proved typical, she would remain apart from her band only a short time, however, perhaps a day or two. As soon as she regained her strength and her foal achieved some proficiency in the management of four legs, she would lead him back to the band. Then, after a brief inspection by the stallion and mares, the little creature would be admitted to their exclusive social unit. But in the meantime, the mare and colt would live apart where both could enjoy freedom from group life and the exacting demands of a domineering stallion.

I was just preparing to photograph the tiny colt when his mother's keen nose, or perhaps her ears, picked up the news of my proximity, and she charged over the hill so suddenly, I thought a brigade of horses was approaching. My heart stopped for a second, and I all but flew from the baby as the wild mare descended the slope in such a headlong rush a minor rock slide followed her. Stones crunched as she swirled round the foal, a move that instantly brought the little creature to his feet. Then she took off with the colt wobbling along behind.

Without waiting to focus, I shot two pictures. Then I left the pair alone. I had no desire to tangle with an angry mother horse. Besides, I could see that the newborn foal was having difficulty maneuvering the rough, rock-strewn ground. As he stumbled up the mountain, his

41

legs sprawled apart comically. But the mare, with an uncanny sense of what was taking place behind her, slowed her pace to a walk.

After a time, she turned and bussed her tired baby with her nose, and he folded to the ground like a dropped marionette. Once again I was impressed to see how his golden coat blended with the desert dust as he all but vanished before my eyes. Had I not known exactly where he was lying, I doubt I would have spotted him.

When the colt was settled, the mare turned and looked back at me with a defiant expression that clearly communicated her intention to attack should I be so foolish as to try to approach. Her colt needed a rest after the short but strenuous uphill climb, and she evidently was going to see that he got it.

When I did not follow the mare seemed reassured that I would not molest her baby. But I had no intention of leaving. Though I did not relish the notion of being pummeled to dust by an outraged mother mustang, at the same time I did not want to lose the opportunity of observing and photographing a mare with her newborn foal. So I climbed an adjacent hill until I was on the same level as the pair. A narrow crevasse divided us, putting me only a short distance from the two animals by air, or by telephoto lens. But by overland route the terrain that separated us was long and rough. If the mare was nervous about this new arrangement, at least she made no attempt to move her colt. In fact, she studied me boldly across the chasm, and I, in turn, looked long and hard at her and from time to time spoke reassuring words.

I congratulated myself on my good fortune to be able to study a wild mare at such close range. The female wild horse is extremely high-strung and usually flees at the least sign of anything unusual. And apprehensiveness in one mare is quickly telegraphed to others; almost anything can trigger a stampede! This makes the wild female horse very difficult to approach.

Yet for all their apparent flightiness, certain females perform key roles in the daily life of the band, and a pecking order seems to exist even among members of a harem. Though any mare may signal a retreat, only the lead-mare, or most dominant female, decides the direction and route to be taken. While the stallion stays behind to face the oncoming threat, the lead-mare must adroitly avoid leading the band into man-made traps or dead-end canyons where the animals could be cornered. In the performance of her role, a detailed knowledge of the habitat is essential, and, as a consequence, most lead-mares have some age advantage on their harem-sisters.

I have watched a good lead-mare lose me, her pursuer, by crossing a seemingly unassailable ridge or by galloping down a precipitous canyon trail that looked as if it might present peril even to mountain goats. Yet, when pressured by an enemy, wild horses do not hesitate in their headlong flight; they follow the dominant female even along the most precarious routes. Bands that have survived to the present time, in spite of man's weaponry and mechanized advantages, probably have been led by the most dauntless females.

How or why a particular female casts herself in the role of the lead-mare is a mystery. Pelligrini once told me that he once witnessed a fierce fight between two mares. However, it is unlikely that female rank is settled by force; otherwise mare battles would have been observed more frequently.

In his thesis, Pelligrini gives evidence that mares not only respect order of rank during an emergency, but observe protocol in routine matters as well. When watering at a spring which is too small to accommodate all the animals at one time, the most dominant female, along with her colt, will drink first. After about five minutes, she moves away and the next most dominant mare approaches to drink. (I suspect the second mare in rank is the female most closely bonded to the lead-mare.) The stallion, on the other hand, stands guard and waters last after all the mares have drunk their fill. Should he attempt to drink out of turn, Pelligrini asserts, the lead-mare will drive him back.

Because of their natural shyness, my observations of wild mares were not often at close range; consequently, I was delighted to spend a whole day watching the dun-colored mare whose reluctance to move her weary foal had rooted her to one spot. During most of the afternoon the colt slept, while the mare stood over him and I looked on. Time, it seemed to me, gradually slowed its tempo to be more in harmony with the new life that gently throbbed at the feet of the wild mare. As I sat quietly on the mountainside, a sense of peace banished my usual compulsive drive to scribble notes and take pictures. I recalled Walt Whitman's line:

> I think I could turn and live with the animals, they are so placid
> and self-contain'd;
> I stand and look at them long and long.

It was a beautiful day in my life.

Finally, the colt struggled to his feet and searched for the nipple, but the effort of drinking exhausted him quickly and he tumbled back into the sage for another long rest. His mother guarded him so solicitously I decided to call her Angel.

I wondered what kind of a future Angel's colt would face. If he enjoyed the normal life expectancy of a wild horse, he might live slightly over two decades. Would there still be room for wild horses in America in his lifetime? With the population burgeoning and America consuming resources at an ever-accelerating rate, how long before our open spaces will be devoured and our wild animals deprived of their last retreats?

As I sat pondering the probable effects of what is, euphemistically, called "progress" on our dwindling wildlife, I suddenly noticed a male horse wending his way up the mountain toward the dun mare. He was a stocky red-brown animal with a faded gray mane and tail and four white stockings. He appeared to carry some draft blood; his feet were large and his back long, unlike the typical mustang whose feet are small and whose short back, like many of his Arab-Barb ancestors, often lacks a final lumbar vertebra.

In a few minutes, the big horse pulled up to within a few feet of Angel and her colt and slowly turned broadside to them. I supposed this action to be some kind of conciliatory gesture. But whatever he may have been trying to communicate, Angel took absolutely no notice of him. The two horses simply stood quietly together facing outward at right angles, while seemingly ignoring one another.

The stockinged male was not oblivious to my existence, however, although my presence across the narrow divide did not put him to flight. He, as had the mare, seemed to realize what a long lead he had on me, and he used this advantage to satisfy his curiosity. In fact, he fixed on me such a steadfast gaze, I began to wonder how long the animal could stand stock-still and stare. But the question that really mystified me was what he was doing at Angel's foaling site.

As a rule, the male ignores the departure of a pregnant female from his harem and patiently awaits her voluntary return. Sometimes a mare with a new colt may choose to live apart for several months, but this is unusual. Ordinarily, a female will foal and return to the harem within a day or two. I had heard reports, however, of stallions retrieving their mares a short time after they had delivered their colts, and I wondered if I were about to witness this now.

But the white-stockinged male made no attempt to drive Angel and her foal anywhere. On the contrary, he seemed to be totally content just to stand beside her. I began to suspect that Angel was the only member of his harem and that he had joined her in her private foaling place out of desperate loneliness, horses being the social animals that they are.

I soon had to reject this theory, however, when I spied two black mares, each with an ebony colt, peering down at me from behind a rocky crest a few hundred yards above. I climbed the mountain to spy on the band at closer range and found them unattended by a stallion, a fact that led me to conclude that they belonged to the white-stockinged male. Yet for some strange reason, the stallion made no attempt to drive the dun mare and her colt toward them. While the black mares waited, unguarded and easy prey for any roving stud band, the big male remained by the side of Angel and her newborn foal.

Another idea occurred to me. If Angel were not this stallion's sole mare, perhaps the explanation for his strange behavior rested on the possibility that she was his favorite. Was he willing to risk losing all the others in order to protect his deeper interest in this one? In view of how cohesive two bonded horses can be, I had to regard this explanation as viable.

Then still another thought struck me. Perhaps the dun-colored female was actually a stranger to the stockinged stallion. He, like myself, may have discovered her by chance, alone and in a vulnerable plight, detached from her mate and restrained by a newborn foal. And perhaps in his own fashion he was striking up an acquaintance with her and awaiting the time when she would readily be driven to his harem.

If so, I had observed still another means by which males may sometimes acquire females and augment their harems without doing battle with other males. Perhaps some opportunistic

44

stallions pick up mares that have gone off alone to foal. Or was this technique only the ingenious tactic of one brown male with white stockings and a gray mane?

Later, when I discussed Angel with a local wild-horse enthusiast, the Reverend Floyd Schweiger, he told me that due to her unusual coloration, he had not only noticed the mare I described, but had identified her over several seasons. He was quite emphatic that she did not belong in the harem of the white-stockinged stallion, so perhaps my second guess was correct.

I never learned what happened to Angel or to the male I had come to regard as her suitor. Though I diligently looked for the pair over the next week, I failed to locate them. Nor did I ever again witness a male abandoning his harem to remain beside a mare and her newborn foal. However, wild mares are very discreet in the selection of a foaling site, and I have rarely been fortunate enough to run across any mare immediately after she has delivered a colt.

Many people have told of seeing a barren female in the company of a new mother and foal at the birth site. In southern Nevada I, myself, have witnessed one such an instance, and even managed to photograph it. At that time, I failed to question the widespread notion that the female who accompanies the mare and foal does so out of a frustrated urge for motherhood. But after giving the phenomenon more thought, I have now come to the conclusion that the two females probably remain together because they are so closely bonded.

Nevertheless, the motive power of the maternal drive in wild horses should not be minimized. Many mares are plainly "colt crazy," and a few will even try to steal the baby of a harem-sister. I once saw a mare with an adopted orphan whom she allowed to nurse along with her own offspring to the detriment of all three animals. But the most dramatic story of frustrated maternity I ever witnessed occurred during my last trip to Sykes Valley, and the leading lady in the incident was a bright blue creature I called Blue Mare.

Blue Mare was such an unbelievable shade of indigo she actually rivaled the mountain bluebirds that flashed in and out of the wild horse bands early in the morning. The other two female members of the harem were also unusually beautiful. Both were pale buckskins, or sandy duns, with black manes and tails. But the black mane and tail of one were streaked with white, giving her the elegant look of a fashionable lady who has had her hair frosted at the beauty parlor. These lovely mares were ruled by a common-looking dark bay stallion with a white star and a mealy muzzle.

When first I saw this harem in the spring of 1970, none of the mares had a colt; but sixteen months later, when I revisited Sykes Valley, two foals were among them, a bay and a buckskin. I was excited and eager to know which of the three mares were the mothers of the two rollicksome fillies that circled the band, bucking and kicking. I hoped that Blue Mare had given birth to one; for, though neither filly was blue, any one of Blue Mare's progeny might carry a recessive gene for her color, and I was anxious for her incredible shade to be passed on to posterity.

It was a windy September day and I sat down on the ground to await the moment of truth when the two fillies would tire of their exhausting game, grow hungry, and run to their respective mothers to nurse. While I was waiting, I began to notice that some of the horse bands were violating what had been their summer range boundaries during my previous visit. Several bands had bunched up at one end of the valley. The change in weather, perhaps, was signaling them to shift their range, an important factor in the relief and ultimate health of the land they used.

But during my absence, a government fence had been constructed across the full length of Sykes Valley and this barrier now restricted the horses from moving up the mountain. It also prevented the horses that lived higher up in the range from making trips to the valley where water was more abundant.

I could hardly control my indignation over the well-meaning but misguided project. The fence had been constructed across the wilderness area because a portion of the long abandoned Sykes homestead had been deeded to a private owner. The rest, however, had reverted to the federal government around the turn of the century. But the owner of the private section, as it happened, was an individual who for many years had urged the federal agency in charge of all public lands in the Pryor Mountains to protect and preserve the herd of wild horses that inhabited the range. In fact, once he had even joined with others in a court action to prevent that government agency from carrying out a plan to dispose of all the mustangs. Had it not been for this action, all the Pryor Mountain wild horses would long ago have been rounded up and destroyed.

Now, however, that the federal bureau had finally acceded to public pressure and had designated thirty-three thousand acres of the mountain range as a wild-horse sanctuary, one of its first acts had been to erect this fence to protect its new charges from one of the mustangs' most outspoken supporters! As a result, many of the wild horses had been confined unnaturally and restrained from shifting their ranges, and others had been cut off from water.

Ironically, the boondoggle fence had inadvertently benefited a few animals. The wild horses that it had excluded from the new government sanctuary and that were now confined to a privately owned wilderness at least had been spared the indignity of being rounded up by federal agents and tattooed with a government brand. For after finally reversing its negative position on the issue of wild horses, the federal agency in charge had begun to take absurd precaution to protect "their" animals from poachers.

For the moment at least, as I sat watching the antics of the two young fillies at play, my indignation over the fence and branding temporarily subsided. In spite of myself, I could not help but be amused by them. At approximately four months of age, they had achieved an amazing degree of independence. At half time in their game, they did not bother to return to their mothers, but quickly nibbled on some grass and resumed their sport. However, I knew it would be only a matter of time before the pair would seek milk. While I waited impatiently, I tried to guess which colt belonged to which mare. The buckskin, I finally decided, belonged to the mare with the streaks in her mane. The bay, perhaps, was the baby of Blue Mare.

At long last the two young animals grew tired of their game and cantered to their respective mothers to suckle. But neither ran to Blue Mare. Incorrectly I surmised that Blue Mare had failed to foal. I hoped that she was not barren.

Suddenly, some horses to the north spooked and began to run the full length of the valley, heading in my general direction. The momentum of their panic quickly spread to a neighboring band of horses, and these animals instinctively joined in the stampede. As the two bands veered in a wide arc, they crossed into the range being used by Blue Mare and the members of her band, and in a swirl of dust, they, too, merged with the mob of horses that pounded wildly about the windy valley.

Then, as quickly as the stampede had erupted, it ended, and the three bands separated, each circling back to its starting point. But when Blue Mare returned, a half-grown colt was at her side, and she, quite blatantly, appeared to be herding it along. I rubbed my eyes. Blue Mare had cut out a colt from one of the other bands!

I grabbed my camera just in time to record the confrontation that swiftly developed. One of the bands had already backtracked, and a buckskin stallion, apparently the sire of the colt, was in full display before Blue Mare's mate. While the two stallions postured, the abducted colt blithely trotted over to his real mother, the two stallions relaxed, and the band galloped away. Had I not recorded this fleeting drama with my camera, I might later have doubted that it had taken place.

But I was in for more surprises. No sooner had the horses settled down again than one of the two fillies I had recently been watching at play sidled over to Blue Mare and began to nurse. It was at that moment that I comprehended the full tragic meaning behind Blue Mare's kidnaping act. Blue Mare was producing milk and that could mean only one thing. She had recently borne and lost a foal of her own!

But the most surprising element in this byplay between wild mares was the relaxed attitude of the buckskin female who was the real mother of the filly. Though the foal appeared to show a preference for her own mother, the buckskin mare never made a fuss when her offspring decided to take a supplementary feeding from Blue Mare.

The more time I have spent watching wild horses, the more impressed I have been by the individuality they so often reveal. I have observed more "characters" among the mustangs than I could possibly document in this book. But since diversity is not the easiest subject to explore meaningfully, at first I tried to look for the predictable aspects of wild-horse behavior.

However, though I looked for sameness (the inductive method by its very nature calls for the enumeration of an unlimited number of similar histories), I soon realized that I was actually more interested in the individuality of the animals I watched. In fact, I began to comprehend the magnitude of the role of idiosyncratic behavior in the scheme of things. Diversity is actually the creative element in the evolutionary process; whereas, the conformity we like to measure is merely the "setting" of nature's wild impulses after these have proved successful over long ages of natural selection. But the dynamic energy behind new forms, behind anomalies, behind unique responses, is an immeasurable force that can never be charted or plotted on a graph. It is the mysterious creative energy that animates the universe.

I was grateful to the wild horses for leading me to this concept; a concept which is more profound than any conclusion I might have drawn from the quantitative material I had amassed. I soon realized, however, that what I had discovered for myself was well understood by others. Loren Eiseley, the renowned anthropologist and writer, in describing the potential hidden in nature and flowering in ever greater variety of behavior, writes: "Natural selection is real but at the same time it is a shifting chimera, less a 'law' than making its own law from age to age."*

Sometimes, though, while watching a recalcitrant wild horse whose behavior contradicted all my previous concepts, I felt myself in contact with this awesome chimera.

*The Unexpected Universe (New York, 1964).

2

4

5

8

9

10▶

◀ 11

12

13
14

15

16

17

18

19

23   24

2

25

27

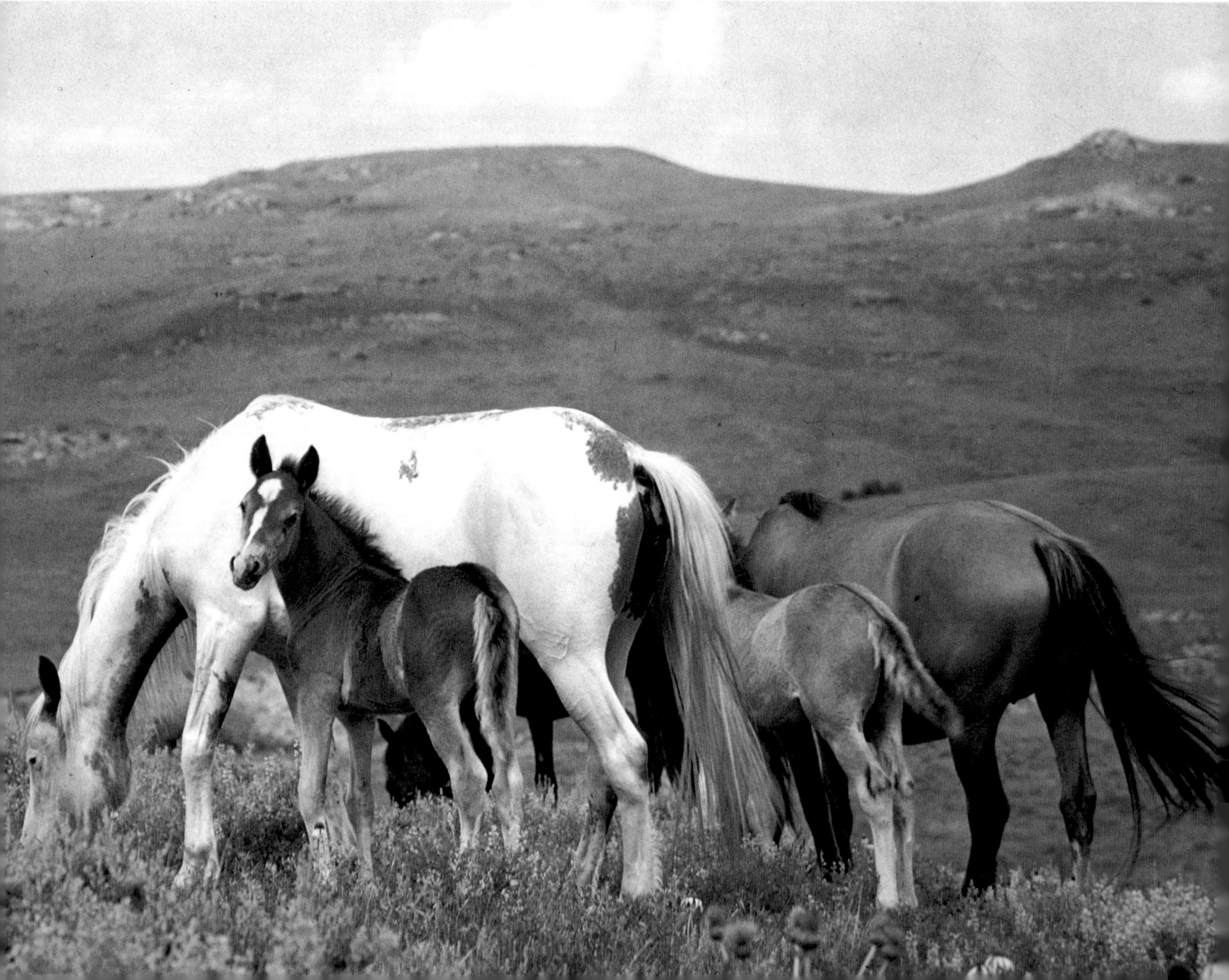

29

30

41   42

43

44

45

46

49
50

51

52

53

54

55

56

The History and Ecology of the Wild Horse

Because the wild horse was introduced into North America by explorers during the sixteenth century, he has frequently been denounced as an interloper and denied legal protection granted to our native animals. However, many who have condemned the wild horse for his alien status are unaware that it was North America that actually spawned the horse and gave this amazing creature to the rest of the world.

Eons ago, not too long after dinosaurs were dragging their tails through swampy bogs, a fox-size creature scampered on four toes and hid from his enemies in the dense jungle foliage that then covered most of the North American continent. This small animal contained in his genetic coding the amazing possibilities of becoming the present-day horse, pony, zebra, donkey, and even mule.

But before he could attain any of these forms, he had to acquire some size and lose three of his four toes. This process did not happen overnight. Millions of years of successful adaptation to changes in weather, the advance and retreat of polar icecaps, the transformation of vegetation from tropical ferns to temperate grasses, the growth of mountains, and the leveling of plains finally wrought the animal we know as *Equus*.

The giant form no longer browsed on twigs of low shrubs as had his primitive ancestors; he had developed a tooth surface that could masticate the new grasses which simultaneously had sprung up under his changing feet. And no longer did he hide from his enemies, for now he could easily outdistance them by running on the overgrown nail of his single remaining toe. His face, too, had altered. His eyes had moved apart, giving him the advantage of extreme wide-angle vision. In fact, all his senses had sharpened, for during his fifty million years of life on this continent he had had to contend with such awesome predators as the saber-toothed tiger and the dire wolf.

Every fragment of the horse's age-old history has been dug up and pieced together from fossil beds in North American soil. Toward the end of the last century, two paleontologists raced to the Bighorn Basin and vied with one another to be the first to find a complete fossil record of equine evolution. The winner was hailed by the scientific world of the late nineteenth century for having assembled the first tangible corroboration of the theory of evolution. Even to the present day, this record of horse evolution remains the best documented fossil evidence of the Darwinian theory.

But the shifting chimera of evolution is a two-headed animal. Not only did the plants, weather, and animals of the continent fashion the horse, but conversely, by his very existence, developing *Equus* had an impact on the forms of life that struggled to evolve around him. By what he ate or did not eat, by whom he fed or did not feed, he influenced the shape of other emerging species.

At the same time, coevolving species are always interdependent. Aside from the obvious relationship that exists between predator and prey, even two plant-eating species that have developed side-by-side require one another's continuing presence in order to eat well. Each occupies a unique ecological niche in the environment and eschews much of the other's diet. Should one disappear, the plants no longer being cropped and eaten by it will quickly overrun the habitat, outcompeting with the plants needed by the surviving species.*

Thus it is reasonable to suppose that the extinction of the native wild horse in North America had severe repercussions. It is not surprising to learn that when he disappeared, a relatively short few thousand years ago, the native American camel and several other species vanished too.

Much mystery surrounds the sudden extinction of the native horse. Most experts believe the early Indians had a hand in it. The fossilized remains of charred horse bones found at Indian cooking sites tell something of the pressure put on the animal by a wave of Asiatic hunters who entered North America some ten thousand years ago. Within two thousand years of their appearance, the wild horse was gone. Though there can be little doubt that these Paleolithic hunters were aided in their grim deed by some natural catastrophe, perhaps an epidemic,† nevertheless, the native horse can accurately be described as the first American species to fall victim to man.

---

*In Africa where a multiformity of fauna exists in profusion, animals thrive better than in North America where misguided wildlife managers often remove one species in the hope of improving conditions for another. Game commissioners, in particular, are guilty of using this management technique in the false belief that they will gain a larger herd of target species for the benefit of hunters.

†*Viz.*, the epidemic of sleeping sickness that recently took such a toll of horses in Texas.

Fortunately, long before the horse had vanished from the scene, some intrepid members of his family succeeded in making the reverse journey across the land bridge that once spanned the Bering Straits, and they reached Asia. There they not only flourished, but in time they spread to North Africa and were domesticated. Thus the handiwork of fifty million years of North American artistry was preserved.

In evolutionary terms, the horse's absence from his homeland was brief. No radical changes of climate, flora, or fauna took place during his sojourn abroad. Consequently, when he was reintroduced, though he himself had been somewhat altered by domestication, the environmental conditions that had fostered his ancestors still remained essentially unchanged. And the horse was not slow to rediscover his natural ecological niche! Almost immediately he began to go wild.

The first horses to be brought back to North America were the tough mounts of the Spanish conquistadores. Paradoxically, this same horse had once been the weapon responsible for the Moors' conquest of Spain in the year 711. But the Spaniards, recognizing the superior worth of the hot-blooded desert steed of their conqueror, had adopted it and even improved the animal by adding a touch of their own Norse Dun. The result was that sixteenth-century Spain possessed the strongest and most able mounts of the period. Basically, however, the animal was still a Libyan Barb (which many authorities say is an offshoot of the oldest known breed, the Arabian).

The horse that had served the Moors so well in their campaign to win the world for Islam now performed equally well for the Spaniards in their quest for gold. In fact, only Spain possessed horses with sufficient stamina to survive the long sea crossing to the New World (hoisted in slings) and upon landing could bear loads one quarter their weight while breaking trail through virgin wilderness. The British and Dutch, lacking such an asset, settled mainly along the seacoasts.

It was largely because of this Andalusian bred Arab-Barb that the conquistadores were able to explore vast tracts of North and South America quickly, conquer the Indians, and plunder all their gold. It is amazing to contemplate the fact that within fifty years of the discovery of America, de Soto had reached the Mississippi, Coronado had trekked across what is now Kansas and New Mexico, and Cortes had conquered Mexico. And all without benefit of maps, roads, or wheels! Superb horses more than anything else were what made these feats possible.

At first, the Indians of the Plains and the Southwest were intimidated by the strange animals that would permit men to ride on their backs. However, the Western tribes were not long in appropriating some of these mounts for themselves. In fact, every chief and brave soon acquired vast herds of stolen stock to help in the buffalo hunt and to ride to war. And this single acquisition, the horse, totally revolutionized the lives of the Plains Indians. Horses represented status and gave the hunting tribes more leisure to invent dances, make moccasins and headdresses, and develop their culture. Even more significantly, horses enabled the Indians to rout the Spaniards and drive them below the Rio Grande. As a result, for the next two centuries until the American frontier pushed across the Great Plains, mounted Indians retained the West for themselves.

During this long period, the horses-gone-wild enjoyed a heyday. The Plains tribes were migratory and careless herdsmen. Though intertribal wars were frequently fought over horses, nevertheless the Indians rarely bothered to picket even their most prized animals, and untold numbers of red-blooded stallions gathered mares and herded them into the wilderness.

These runaways were seldom retrieved. A more practical and interesting method of obtaining fresh stock, which incidentally was already trained, was to ride south into what is now Mexico and raid and ransack Spanish ranches along the border. To save their own lives, the settlers made certain that plenty of horses were always available for the Indians to steal. In fact, the government of New Spain, anxious to protect their harassed settlers, sent a steady flow of mounts northward to placate the horse-hungry Indians. And so during two centuries, thousands upon thousands of Spanish-bred horses were marched to the Rio Grande to be confiscated by Indians. And thousands upon thousands of newly confiscated ponies slipped through the hands of the Indians and found their way to the wild.

No breed was better equipped to withstand the shock of returning to nature than was the Spanish Barb. His desert ancestry served him well in waterless places and where rations were short. Where feed was lush, as on the plains, his population exploded. During the first quarter of the nineteenth century, when American explorers finally began to make their way across the Great Plains, they found enormous herds of wild horses there, commingling with the buffaloes. They assumed these wild horses were indigenous and referred to them as "aboriginal" stock.

It is not surprising that they should have thought so. Most of the horses they saw were dozens of generations and more than two centuries removed from domestication and had completely reverted to wild ways. They mated, fought, played, and defended mares and territory as nature had originally designed them to do.

Moreover, just as nature had intended, the wild horse once again served other species in symbiotic ways. Deer and antelope browsed alongside him, taking advantage of his alert vigilance. And his strength and vigor also benefited many creatures. In freezing weather he unlocked frozen springs by cracking through thick ice with his rock-hard hoofs, and afterward less powerful animals could come to drink. In spring, when these same water holes were clogged with sediment, the horse with his passion for splashing and digging, swept out the debris and brought water to the surface. And in winter, he plowed trails through deep snow, inadvertently releasing any snowbound creatures that might have become trapped on mountain ridges.

Even vegetation seemed to thrive from the horse's return. Unlike the cud-chewing animals, his inefficient digestive system passed whole seeds; thus he replanted his own forage. Moreover, his heavy hoofs trampled air-borne seeds into the ground where they could take root and grow. The Great Plains was a sea of grass.

But the wild horse's heyday was destined to end when American settlers began to straggle out to the Great Plains to tame and settle the prairie wilderness. As the wide strip of land designated as "Indian Territory forever" gradually shrank, so did the horse herds.

The mustang population did enjoy one unexpected boon near the end of the nineteenth century. In the 1870s and 1880s when the last of the Indian wars were fought and the defeated tribes were moved to reservation tracts, their oversized herds of buffalo-runners and war-horses often were not relocated with them. Numbers of these abandoned creatures joined their free-living relatives in the shrinking wilderness.

Many of the Indians' horses were pintos, for the Western tribes dearly loved flashy ponies, and animals not colorful enough for their taste were traded off. Thus each tribe, without resorting to gelding or controlled breeding programs, obtained its own unique strain out of basically similar Spanish Barb stock. The favorite pony of the fighting Cheyenne, for example, was called by them a "Medicine Hat," because the head and the chest of this animal were covered by spots shaped like a bonnet and a shield. Cheyenne warriors believed that horses who were so marked were sacred and would bring them victory in battle.

Undoubtedly, the bonnet and shield markings of the Medicine Hat horses were linked genetically with their strength and mettle; for these animals were indeed dauntless war-horses. Even the settlers feared and respected them and referred to them as "Indian War Bonnets."

In recent years, some Medicine Hat mustangs have been found and retrieved from the wilderness by two brothers, Robert and Ferdinand Brislawn. Over the past fifty years these two men (who are now in their eighties) have searched in remote areas throughout the West for wild horses that still appear to carry pure Spanish Barb blood. With the help of Robert's son, Emmett, many such animals have been captured, registered in their Spanish Mustang Registry, and released again to run free on the Brislawns' four-thousand-acre ranch, a section of which has been designated the "True Blood Reserve." There, the mustangs have been permitted to remain wild, living out their lives in protected freedom.

Most wild horses that have been captured by man have not been so lucky. The decimation of the vast herds of mustangs that once graced our Western landscapes demonstrates perfectly how Americans have traditionally viewed every facet of nature either as a resource to be totally exploited or as a useless impediment to be removed so that the exploitation of some other resource can be better accomplished. In brief, hundreds of thousands of wild horses were rounded up to serve in the Boer War and World War I; hundreds of thousands were captured and converted into chicken feed, fertilizer, and hides; hundreds of thousands were captured and broken into cow ponies; hundreds of thousands were killed by stock-growers who wanted all the free grass on the public lands for their cattle; hundreds of thousands were killed by the United States Grazing Service which, finding itself unable to cope with the human abusers of the vast piece of federal real estate it administered, took action against the wild animal occupants; hundreds of thousands were killed by game managers intent on making more habitat available for target species; and hundreds of thousands were shot by air-borne cowboys merely for the excitement of it. No law protected the wild horse.

From an estimated two million wild horses at the turn of the century, fewer than seventeen thousand remained when I began my research in 1968. These, the toughest and smartest and most unapproachable of the species, had survived by retreating to inaccessible and desolate places not coveted by man. Yet even these holdouts were not safe from man. Though canneries paid next to nothing for horsemeat, men intent on capturing every wild horse in existence went after them in rented planes and labored long hours to construct concealed corrals in which to trap them. Since there could be little or no profit in the "mustanging business," I inquired of some of these individuals why they bothered the remaining horses and was told they did so because the horses were "no good."

From the air, of course, the mustangs could easily be located and stampeded out of their last retreats. Screaming sirens attached to a plane's wings and blasts of buckshot would convince even the most reluctant lead-mare to abandon her home range and lead her band to open country where men waiting in trucks could drive the panicked animals into makeshift corrals. There the survivors could be loaded into trucks and those not too badly injured by the rough herding method shipped to slaughterhouses.

Wild horses were declining at such an accelerating rate by 1970 that experts predicted the mustang would be extinct within the decade. But the reaction of the public and the press to the publication of these facts was heartening. Two weeks after *America's Last Wild Horses* came into print, *The New York Times* picked up the story and carried details of the mustangs' plight on its front page. Immediately, nearly every large newspaper in the country followed suit, and radio and TV programs invited friends of the wild horses to appear and discuss the issue. Within the next six months, the *National Geographic Magazine* carried "On the Track of the West's Wild Horses"; the *Reader's Digest* condensed *America's Last Wild Horses,* and ran a footnote suggesting that concerned readers write their Congressmen; and *Time* magazine devoted its Environment Section to the wild horse.

The result of all this exposure was that Congress was inundated with mail. Senator Henry Jackson reported receiving as many as fourteen thousand letters on the issue during a single week. Needless to say, with public interest at such a pitch, legislation to protect the mustang was introduced and enacted in the Ninety-second Congress. But not a moment too soon. In December 1971, when President Nixon signed P.L. 92–195* into law making it a federal offense

*The final bill was the end product of two excellent measures—one drawn up by Congressman Walter S. Baring in the House and the other by Senators Jackson and Hatfield in the Senate.

to harass or kill a wild horse, fewer than ten thousand mustangs could be counted in scattered bands across eleven Western states. But many of these remaining bands were already too small to be viable and too far-distant from other bands to gain any new recruits. Clearly, when protective legislation was finally enacted, the wild horse was well on his way to becoming extinct for the second time in America.

Though many Congressmen and Senators were astonished at the deluge of mail they received on the wild-horse issue, the public's sentiments hardly surprised me. From that day in May 1968, when I first sighted a band of wild horses and resigned my job to devote the next four years to photographing and writing about them, I have been carrying on a kind of love affair with wild horses.

No sight so thrills me as the silhouette of an arrogant stallion poised atop a ridge. No spectacle so fires my imagination as the *pas de deux* of two stallions in full display. No discovery so moves me as the disclosure that a desert bush conceals a newborn foal. Though words cannot adequately describe either my feelings or the wild horses, Frank Dobie came close when he said that the wild horse was "the most beautiful, the most spirited, and the most inspiriting creature ever to print foot on the grasses of America." And he further added that only true conceivers of freedom, people who yearn to extend freedom to all life, could fully appreciate this animal.

I agree. Perhaps it is because the horse has for so long been cast in the role of man's servant that free horses appear so poignantly beautiful. For I suspect it is freedom that I see when I thrill to a band of wild horses racing across a desert flat, their uncut manes flopping in a kind of counterpoint to their undulating rhythm. Moreover, I suspect it is because the horse-gone-wild, by his very existence, proves that even a lost freedom can be recovered, that so many people responded with such overwhelming support to the cause of the mustangs. For many letter writers admitted that it was unlikely that they would ever see a wild horse; yet they said they wanted to know that wild horses still exist in America.

Thanks to those true conceivers of freedom who asked that freedom be extended to all life, wild horses do still exist in America.

NOTES TO THE PLATES

(1)   A lone gray stallion ambushes and imprisons me while he circles and inspects what is very likely the first human being he has ever seen.

This wild horse is one of several hundred that inhabit a vast military weapons test site in southern Nevada which is off limits to the public. Paradoxically, several decades of isolation from man appears to have benefited wildlife here.

(2)   Three young mares line up beside their mate, an aging but still viable stallion. The mare in the middle reveals her nervousness over my proximity by pawing the ground. Seconds later, the band took flight and vanished into the immense Yellowtail Canyon seen in the background.

(3)   Two young males I dubbed the Juvenile Delinquents stare at me quizzically. Too immature to win and defend their own harems and too old to be retained in their parental bands, the pair has teamed up for companionship.

(4)   Blue Mare and her harem-sisters in flight. The colt in the picture is shared by Blue Mare and the female running beside her.

(5)   The Black King, the most dynamic stallion in the Pryor Mountains, gallops the length of Sykes Valley to head off a stallion who is about to cross his territory.

(6) The Black King and his bevy of brunette beauties. This wild stallion has a predilection for mares of a particular color.

(7) Two stallions separate their respective harems after taking part in a joint stampede. The stallion always trails his mares so he can make a defense against pursuers.

(8) A wild foal spends much time resting, but is ready on an instant's signal to take flight.

(9) A stallion eyes me defiantly while his mares are escaping. He will soon follow, however, before they have outdistanced him too far.

(10) A lonely stallion with neither a harem nor male companions is responsive to my "sweet talk" and hangs around my camp in a southern Nevada mountain range.

SERIES (11–20)

(11) A pinto stallion, sensing the approach of a rival, leaves his mares to investigate.

(12) The approaching palomino stallion, oblivious to the danger ahead, incautiously brings his mare and colt to water.

(13) In a face-down, the two males enact a ritual that is mandatory before every stallion fight. Both perform a display, arching their necks and pawing the ground aggressively. During this phase, either horse has the option of backing down and running away.

(14) In this case, however, neither horse will acknowledge defeat in advance of an actual battle. A long squeal from the palomino signals the start of the fight, and both horses instantly whirl and kick one another with their powerful hind legs.

(15) As the battle escalates, so do the horses. Stallion fights, for the most part, are waged in an upright position.

(16 & 17) The two horses lunge for one another's necks and fence with their sharp front hoofs.

106

(18)   Though the horses are evenly matched, the palomino is handicapped by the fact that he is on alien turf. In most instances, it is the intruder who becomes intimidated.

(19)   When the palomino backs down and starts to retreat, the pinto rears and celebrates his victory by waving his forefeet in the air. Neither horse incurred serious injury.

(20)   The defeated palomino moves to an unclaimed portion of the stream to drink and assuage his injured feelings.

(21)   The most serious survival problem for wild horses is finding water. In arid sections of the West, man has claimed, diverted, or fenced most viable streams and springs. Wild horses often must dig for water. Few wild horses have access to such abundant water as the animals in this picture.

(22)   The wild horses running across this isolated Nevada test site illustrate how deceptive a desert landscape can be. Though the expanse appears flat, it is furrowed and conceals animals as large as wild horses.

SERIES (23–28)

(23)   A gray and a black stallion challenge one another for control of a harem.

(24)   During their display, the two males press their faces together in an eyeball-to-eyeball confrontation.

(25)   Though the black appears to back down, instead of leaving, he runs to the front of the harem line-up and usurps the place of the lead-mare.

(26)   In the meantime, the victorious gray has claimed the dominant position at the end of the line. But when he spots his adversary up front, he rushes forward and overtakes him.

(27)   While the mares wait patiently, the two males once again vie for possession of the harem.

(28)   A Medicine Hat mare and her foal live in protected freedom on the "True Blood Mustang Reserve" near Oshoto, Wyoming. Horses marked like this pinto mare were once believed to be sacred by the Cheyenne Indians.

The "True Blood Mustang Reserve" was established by two brothers, Robert and Ferdinand Brislawn, in an attempt to retrieve and protect wild horses that still appear to carry the blood of the mounts of the sixteenth-century Spanish conquistadores.

(29)   Newborn foals that have been brought back to the harem a few days after birth.

(30)   Twinning, though rare in the horse family, is not uncommon in the herd of wild horses inhabiting the Pryor Mountains along the Montana-Wyoming border. Only one of this pair survived.

(31)   A red roan mare and her beautiful foal run across unturned prairie sod. The foal, a filly, will change color as she matures.

(32)   Angel, a wild mare who has left her harem to give birth, conceals her newborn foal under a bush.

(33)   On hot days when insects plague them, wild horses climb to high altitudes to catch the breezes. Cattle are not so intelligent and commonly head for brushy areas where insects are thickest.

(34)   To protect their hides from stings and bites, wild horses cover themselves with mud and dirt.

(35)   Caked with earth, this stallion is now well insulated from flies.

(36)   Wild horses perform many cooperative acts. To fight flies, this band has formed a wheel and all the horses are switching their tails in unison. The colt's stub tail, however, is not a very effective fly swatter.

(37)· Three of the Black King's look-alike mares shield one another's bodies from flies.

(38)   Two bands join together in a stampede on a windy September day in Sykes Valley.

(39)   The distinct black stripes on the back and around the legs of this horse reveal its long mustang lineage. Horses revert to this primitive pattern after being wild for many generations.

(40)   The wild horses of the Pryor Mountains are renowned for their vivid and unusual colors; yet they are surprisingly well camouflaged. Here a brilliant blue horse blends with junipers and mountain mahogany.

(41)   A wild horse, still wearing his winter coat in April, climbs to cooler altitudes in the Pryor Mountains. In winter, wild horses must survive temperatures sometimes as low as thirty below zero.

(42)   Migrating elk graze in winter pasture near the Grand Teton Range. Unlike the wild horse, the elk is a target animal and consequently it receives preferential treatment from state game managers intent on building up large trophy herds for the benefit of hunters. When wild horses and game animals are believed to be in competition, wild horses have been sacrificed.

(43)   Horses in the middle altitudes of the Pryor Mountains have difficulty finding water. These two studs have entered an abandoned mine shaft to drink.

(44)   A bird drinks from a wild horse's hoofprints, demonstrating the interdependence of life.

(45)   Wild horses dig sediment out of a spring, thereby opening it for their own use and making water available for other species as well.

(46)   A view of the Bighorn Basin from the Pryor Mountains. Thirty-three thousand acres of this mountain range have been designated a wild-horse refuge.

(47)   A stallion picks up the scent of a mare in heat and responds by raising his head and flaring his lips.

(48)   A Medicine Hat mare and her foal before a summer hailstorm. On the treeless Great Plains, wild horses cannot shelter from the elements.

(49)   Blackie, a young stallion, elongates his neck and herds Buck, his male companion, as if he were a female. While they are maturing, young studs band together and practice the skills they will someday need to gather and defend harems.

(50)   The Juvenile Delinquents console one another after being defeated in a battle with a mature stallion.

(51)   Blackie rears and paws the air during a mock battle with Buck. Blackie was later shot by a Wyoming game official who objected to him drinking from a spring where antelope watered.

(52) Two stallions pull the mane of a low-ranking male yearling in a symbolic assertion of dominance over him.

(53) Buck clouts the Black King during a five-way horse fight.

(54) Buck, a member of the Bandito stud band, spends an afternoon visiting another pair of young bachelors, the Juvenile Delinquents.

(55) A white buckskin stallion in southern Nevada stares me down while his mare and foal turn to flee. The agile colt jumps a bush on the turn.

(56) The furry feet of this wild horse hint at draft-horse ancestry. His short back, on the other hand, is a sign that Barb blood may also be present. The small stature of this animal is no indication of inferior stock, but is an adaptation to his meager habitat. Nature has scaled him down to be in proportion to the available forage. Misguided efforts to upbreed wild horses through the introduction of domestic stallions invariably have disastrous results.

(57) A band of wild horses high in Nevada's Wassuk Range head for California. Mount Grant is in the background.

(58) After his mare and foal have gained sufficient lead-time, a white buckskin stallion turns to follow them.

(59) Blue Mare herds a kidnaped colt into her band.

(60) Young Blackie, brimming with vitality, moves across Sykes Valley in full display.

REFERENCES

Dobie, J. Frank. *The Mustangs*. New York: Branhill House, 1934.

Eiseley, Loren. *The Unexpected Universe*. "The Inner Galaxy." New York: Harcourt, Brace & World, 1964.

Lorenz, Konrad. *On Aggression*. New York: Harcourt, Brace & World, 1963.

Pelligrini, Steven W. "Home Range, Territoriality and Movement Patterns of Wild Horses in the Wassuk Range of Western Nevada." Thesis submitted at the University of Nevada, January 12, 1971.

Portmann, Adolf. *Animals as Social Beings*. New York: The Viking Press, 1961.

Ryden, Hope. *America's Last Wild Horses*. New York: E.P. Dutton, 1970.

Ryden, Hope. "On the Track of the West's Wild Horses". *National Geographic Magazine*, January 1971.

Scott, John Paul. *Animal Behavior*. Chicago: The University of Chicago Press, 1958.

Simpson, George Gaylord. *Horses*. Garden City, New York: Doubleday & Co., 1950.

Date Due
